Monsters: Addiction, Hope, Ex-girlfriends, and Other Dangerous Things

Monsters

Addiction, Hope, Ex-girlfriends, and Other Dangerous Things

BY

Daniel van Voorhis

Virtue In The Wasteland Books
An imprint of New Reformation Publications

Monsters: Addiction, Hope, Ex-girlfriends, and Other Dangerous Things

© 2017 Daniel van Voorhis

Published by:
Virtue In The Wasteland Books
PO Box 54032
Irvine, CA 92619-4032

Publisher's Cataloging-In-Publication Data
(Prepared by The Donohue Group, Inc.)

Names: Van Voorhis, Daniel, 1979–
Title: Monsters : addiction, hope, ex-girlfriends, and other dangerous things /
    by Daniel van Voorhis.
Description: Irvine, CA : Virtue in the Wasteland Press, an imprint of New
    Reformation Publications, [2017]
Identifiers: ISBN 978-1-945500-78-7 (hardcover) | ISBN 978-1-945500-76-3
    (softcover) | ISBN 978-1-945500-77-0 (ebook)
Subjects: LCSH: Van Voorhis, Daniel, 1979- | College teachers—Biography. |
    Coming of age. | Compulsive behavior. | Man-woman relationships. | LCGFT:
    Autobiographies. | Black humor.
Classification: LCC LA2317.V36 A3 2017 (print) | LCC LA2317.V36 (ebook) |
    DDC 370.92—dc23

Virtue In The Wasteland Books is an imprint of New Reformation
Publications, exploring goodness, truth and beauty in our complex culture.

Printed in the United States of America

To Beth Anne

Contents

Acknowledgments

"Has writing this book destroyed you?" My friend Dan Siedell asked me this just as I was finishing this manuscript. My answer: "Absolutely." Writing this has been a four-year process that has been as painful and arduous as anything I have done. It started out as an anonymous and somewhat cheeky and ironic book. I then started to take it more seriously and was convinced to put my name on it. The book was suggested by friends who listened to my stories and thought I should write them down. A number of the stories in this book have never been told out of embarrassment. I floated the idea originally by students I had taken to Scotland as a summer class at Concordia University Irvine. These students were Cate, Avary, Rachel, Katie, Julianna, David, Nick, Lauren, Kirstin, Melissa, Jamie, and Sandy. Other students that helped were my string of hardworking TAs. Jennifer Wolf was my TA in the worst years of my addiction and covered me far too often when I was too drunk or hungover to get to class. She quit because covering for me became too much for an undergraduate trying to finish college. She remained a good student and help through her graduation. My other TAs who helped immensely were Christina, Josh, Elyssa, Emily, Katie, Amanda, Brook, Sam, Taylor, and Jourden.

At Concordia I have a number of friends whose influence has been immeasurable. My old boss, Tim, was a model of quiet resolve, conviction, and pragmatism. CJ made sure that we kept the pedal down academically. John could frustrate the hell out of me, but his intentions were usually good, and he was one of the few who knew about my addiction and recovery from the beginning. There are many others, but I want to point out my good friend Adam as the friendliest dark cloud I've ever known. His commitment to his family and ability to brush off work is something many of us at the university couldn't do. And Jacque, I once considered her a nuisance in getting my curriculum plan passed for the history department. As I grew older, I recognized her for what she actually was: a cherished colleague, an academic, and most important, a kind woman whose door was always open to the young punk professor across the suite.

Kyle, Ryan, and Anne are my oldest friends, and despite my long periods of silence, they have remained a great encouragement and source of both memories of events I could not remember and earlier editorial suggestions. Their friendship through my darkest years (despite my hiding as much as I could from them) saved my life. My time in Scotland could have ended disastrously, but I was able to keep my sanity on account of my good friends Paul, Stuart, Graeme, Sara, Heather, Mike, and many others. Bruce, my supervisor, has been one of my greatest supporters and a role model of scholarship and humanity.

Despite some of the dark family parts in the book, I have been fortunate enough to have several people come alongside me, help to guide me, and serve as role models: the Hodels, the Longs, and the Brothwells. Donald and Elizabeth Brothwell have been as close to me as anyone. I consider them both parental figures and friends.

This book would not exist without the friendship of Kurt and Debi Winrich. I cannot say enough about their tireless support of our projects. They possess a generosity, kindness, and selflessness that is rare. The other people behind 1517—Jim, Dave, Rod and the rest of the board—have been ardent supporters and friends. My colleagues the Keiths have been tireless in their work and support of the projects Scott oversees. Scott has been the ideal colleague and boss. This job is truly amazing because of the atmosphere he has created. Thanks to Steve and Ted, Stacie, Sam, Caleb, Joy, Karen, and our newest pal, Doug. Steve Byrnes quietly did all the things most people don't notice when you publish a book. He created the ViW imprint, arranged for the early days of press and media, and worked with the whole team to make sure that things ran smoothly.

To some of the characters in the book who didn't submit footnotes, thank you for letting me tell my story and for being a part of it. Anyone in this book who I did not get the chance to ask for footnotes or responses can contact me, and we can add notes to the book section on danvanvoorhis.com, and if we are lucky enough to get a second edition, we can go from there!

It would be impossible for me to convey and write everything that my good friend and cohost of the *Virtue in the Wasteland* podcast Jeff Mallinson has done for me. He has encouraged everything I have done from writing this book, to leaving my job at the university, thinking deeply about spirituality and mostly everything we cover on the show. The last four years have been pushed forward by his tireless work and ability to maneuver between political landmines both socially and professionally. This book would not be finished if it wasn't for him. Stacie, his wife, has been gracious and kind in ways that have been a model of selflessness.

My wife, Beth Anne, and sons, Coert and Raymond, felt the biggest brunt of my writing this book. I was often gone or brooding and stressed when I was at home. "When is Daddy going to be finished?" they asked innumerable times. Often I have been dissuaded to fall into harmful activities because of them. The last chapter serves as a kind of letter to them. Writing this book has been more influenced by my wife, Beth Anne, than anyone. My gratitude for her and her support and love is impossible to express fully. She endured the last nine years of my addiction and then the tenuous early years of my sobriety, and toward the end of writing this book, we separated and almost got a divorce. She has given me the perspective and support that made this book possible. She has taken her vows seriously in sticking together in sickness and health. This book is dedicated to her.

Foreword

All Rights Reserved, All Wrongs Reversed

A Polish philosopher once remarked that forewords to books are like entryways to houses, except a house needs an entryway.

Some find it even graver a sin to include caveats or excuses to begin a book. You are very welcome to skip the forewords and self-conscious caveats. You might just want to jump into the first chapter and then, if you wish, come back and read this later. That's fine with me. In this age of digital printing (I assume some of you will be reading this on tablets or phones or some kind of e-device), you should be able to excise sections of a book completely. Perhaps if you had your own editor, they could send you books with the offensive or banal parts cut out. If you don't care for the vulgarity, you could get a version that substitutes "dang" and "fiddlesticks" for the more earthy language. If you would prefer less spirituality, or if you would like to replace my religious tribe with the religion of your choosing, your personal editor could hit ctrl+F and switch out the name of one deity for another. For a nominal fee, I would be happy to send you a copy tailored to your liking. Welcome to the future. Everything is for you! After all, it is you the reader for whom this book has been written. You are making my life complete by playing the receptor to my transmitter.

Except, I never thought about this project with you in mind. And not just you specifically but you generally. I started this work almost four years ago without you in mind. I was white-knuckling sobriety and trying to keep a step ahead of both professional and personal disaster. I wasn't trying to teach or entertain. I was trying to figure myself out. Writing this down was in my bones.

Musicians make music because it is in their bones, and unless they are bound by contractual stipulations that prevent them, they make albums to see what their melodies and words and production will sound like. I am writing this experimental autobiography for similar reasons. I have had no success in this genre. (My graduate work was spent looking at the lives of others and how they wrote about themselves, but that dissertation is bone-dry boring.) I have been working for years on this thing that is now in front of you. It has been a series of notes, scribbles on legal pads, Word documents, and now something printed by actual people who thought it a good enough idea to let others in on all of this. And by "all this," I mean the peculiar autobiographical experiment. It is an experiment because it deals with memory, addiction, suicide, and hope. The kind of hope I have been battling my entire life. It is a strange story because I was ready to kill myself. A couple of times. But it was the strange mix of music and girls and an inner monologue created by a mental illness that led me from the edge to the guy who is probably right now, as you are reading these very words, horrified at what you will think of the whole project and totally cool with it all as well. I don't want to ruin the end for you, but things work out all right.

Writing, or recording an album, or doing anything creative with words or sounds or shapes has a parallel with getting a girl to like you. (Music and girls are perhaps the two most prominent things in this story.) You want your album to feel timeless and meticulously made but also with a bit of devil-may-care coolness, like you just threw it together. The cover should be neither too artsy nor too clever. You want to sound like this band and not like that band, but you want to be original. You want to be the band that people don't just put on in the background, but listen to with intent. But by the time you are done working out the songs and artwork, a band slightly more polished puts out the album that overshadows yours. It's the same with being a guy trying to impress a girl. You want to come off as self-assured and confident. You want to look suave and make things look effortless. At the same time, you are scared out of your mind and uneasy and sweaty and ready to bolt for the door. Getting person X to like you is both the best and worst idea you've ever had. You have to strike the balance between nice, slightly dangerous, funny without trying too hard, having good posture, pleasant breath, and a decent haircut that makes it appear as if you neither just got it, nor need one . . . and by the time you've made the list of things to do in your head, she has walked away. Or she started dating Mike Simpson or Jake Stevens. The Mike Simpsons and Jake Stevens of the world always get the girl. At least it seems like that. Maybe those guys are deeply troubled and miserable; I don't wish that upon them, but I suspect even they have undesirable qualities. But I wouldn't know. They haven't written their books yet.

With all of this out of the way (or perhaps if you haven't skipped the section yet), I should probably start with some kind of foreword. This is usually done with bold letters, center justified, that read:

Foreword, Cont.

But I think it is more fair to call this:

(Optional) Preface #1

Historians are trained to explain the past through the intersections of people, events, and ideas. The perils of historical writing are legion, but it does not make it a fool's errand to try to understand the past. Even the tiniest things can have an impact on future generations. The insignificant, the outsider, and the lowly have stories that, albeit hard to reconstruct, change things.

This project is based on a historian taking the tools of his trade and turning them on himself.

While this story is not without parallels (there are probably millions who have had similar families, friends, stories, strife, and tragedy), this is the story of *one* of those people. Told by a historian. About himself.

My story runs from a murky past filled with miscreants for relatives to a peculiar and short-lived career in show business, mental illness of a fairly serious order, alcoholism, and eventually stumbling into a PhD and a job as a professor. The story is not filled with bullshit aphorisms, nor is it some Trojan horse designed to argue for abstinence or some kind of morality leading to a victory-filled life. In fact, I would like to think that while you read this, you are enjoying a fine beverage and take my story as exactly that: my story. If it makes you evaluate aspects of yourself or a loved one, I assume the story has resonated in some way. Feel free to do with this story as you wish, but remember this is just my story.

The introduction is probably a bad place for a caveat, seeing that you may have already paid for the book and have just started to read it. I'll warn you that I am quite afraid that this book will be seen by many as too religious and by others as not religious at all. A sheep in wolf's clothing or the other way around. One of the major themes throughout this book is radical grace. Graciousness from friends, spouses, kids, and the guy who I was convinced was some made-up sky wizard that people prayed to for cash. Don't worry though, the religion in this book is more Johnny Cash than Pat Boone. It's less Kirk Cameron and more guys who have taught for centuries about time and history and blood and splinters. If you don't feel like "getting religion," don't worry. If you're looking for a theological treatise, I'm afraid this is not the book you are looking for.

It would be easier to tell the story anonymously or to wait until everyone had died and have someone else put the facts together posthumously without fear of repercussion.

But that's part of what makes this story different.

I have entrusted a few of the characters in this story (my wife, former girlfriends, etc. . . .) to interject periodically throughout the text. They stay in the middle part of the book, for the most part. It is only the ex-girlfriends in the title of this book who can speak for themselves. And so I have let them. If anything starts to sound like bullshit, these contributors get to have their say of how the story looked from the outside. Going inside your own mind and guts messes you up a bit, as well as skews the story. So giving all these characters from the story the footnotes helps the veracity of the stories. This was an open-sourced autobiography.

As with anything that claims to document "real life," there are a number of questions that inevitably pop up. How real is real? Is this just "based on a true story?"

I will vow to you this: the stuff I am writing about actually happened. Some things are easier to know for certain. Certain things are filtered through my brain, which was semipickled by vodka for many years. I am, however, and for whatever it matters, a professional historian. I deal with the nature of biography and autobiography. I am "trained" to read first-person accounts with a healthy skepticism.

I once gave a talk to a number of younger folks about something (I really can't remember), but it seemed germane to tell them the saddest story I could think of. So I made one up. I made up a super tragic story about my friend Kyle and Char and had pictures of them on PowerPoint and had kids crying about the injustices of this story of cruel fate. Once they were sufficiently worked up, I told them it was all a lie. They were not happy being manipulated. But I asked them if they don't regularly consume media and stories designed to evoke tears. Don't we all watch tragedies? Don't we all cry when Barbara Hershey's character in *Beaches* dies and Bette Midler has to take care of the now motherless child? (I was very young and emotional; I bawled my eyes out.) We all have those fictional stories we go back to for catharsis. But we go in knowing that it isn't true. And so we are cool with it. If we go in thinking it is true only to learn that it was falsified, we are angry. If we know it is fiction from the beginning, we can suspend disbelief.

Part of the genesis of this book was wondering if I could turn the tools of my trade on myself. Biography is hard to verify sometimes, and autobiography seems the more "trustworthy" genre. But I wonder, having written this, if that is the case. It is also why I have had so many people read the manuscripts and asked some to add footnotes that I have promised to not edit.

Does it matter if this is true? Yes. And this *is* a true story of addiction and hope and girls and my love of '80s power ballads and my complicated religious convictions. It will hopefully entertain, probably alienate, possibly educate, and most definitely serve as a kind of historical experiment and confessional for me, your guide on a tour midway through my life.

(Recommended) Preface #2

But before we get to the actual foreword, I'd like to ask if it would be OK if I lay down some ground rules for the reading of this book.

This is the ultimate caveat, and you, of course, are free to tell me to scram and skip to the foreword. These rules will hopefully let me tell you the spirit in which the book is intended and head off a few complaints that you might have.

Rule #1: This book might not be for you. Really, you might have had it recommended, or you might know me or a friend of mine and think you should really read this because you want to see what the fuss is about. But feel free to ditch the book at any point. I do this to about half the books I pick up. No hard feelings.

Rule #1.1: In realizing the book is not for you, you still might want to read it or parts of it. Perhaps you are related to me or you had me as a professor or you are just curious about it. When I started writing this a few years ago, it wasn't written for anyone. And then, when I first started pitching it, it was aimed at a particular audience, and then as I thought more about it, it morphed into a book for a different audience. To tell you the truth, I have no idea to whom this book is supposed to relate. I cohost a podcast with my good friend Dr. Jeff Mallinson, and we have been pretty successful by some metrics, but we have always admitted that the show might be for no one, or everyone—it depends on how you choose to listen.

Rule #2: You are, of course, free to be critical of anything written, but be forewarned that there will be earthy language in this book. It's not *Fifty Shades of Grey* inappropriate, as I was physically and mentally unable to do anything but awkwardly fumble my way through the parts of the relationships where stuff usually happens. Rather, it is the best way I know how to write about real things and how they feel, or felt at that time. You might have had the idea put in your head at some point that people only use profanity when they lack the vocabulary to use more appropriate words. B—S—, language serves a number of purposes and is changing from context to context. They didn't use the word "pregnant" on *I Love Lucy*, and the term "sucks" made *The Simpsons* a target for almost every coalition for suitable standards for the friendly family.

Rule #3: All this is true insofar as we can judge things to be true or false. Everything is as true as I know it to be. The first story in the chapter about my wife was completely misremembered. So much so that it could have changed the point of the story and the way chapters happened. (But my wife does clarify and retell the story as it happened.) There are things I have misremembered, I am sure, but nothing that distorts the story. And where I have misremembered, that alternate reality that I assume is true has become part of the narrative that I believe to be true and has thus shaped subsequent events.

Rule #4: There is no ulterior motive to me writing this (or none that I recognize). I have talked about this project with my therapist and tried to get him to tell me the real reason I am doing this. He tells me it is because I want to. He insists that it is like a musician sitting down with an instrument or an artist a canvas. Except this will take longer to get through. I am not trying to gain sympathy, or to win fame or become fabulously wealthy, or to get you to believe what I believe. Of course, I would like all of those things, but this project was born out of a despair to write. And thus most of it was written when it was going to be either never published, published under a pseudonym, or heavily edited. Publishing this as it is might do me more harm than good (on some scale), but ultimately, this is a creative work of catharsis using the only real tools I have.

Rule #5: Please understand that beneath everything, the last part of my life has been spent within the community of the Christian church, more particularly the Protestant brand and the Lutheran blend. It would be inauthentic to try to write this without having that play a part in the book, as it has played a major part in my life. However, to write this as a kind of testimony is not my intent (and it might not read like one, at all). If you're familiar with the lingo of the twenty-first-century evangelical church, I am one of those "backsliding" Christians. I have a hard time getting into some of the things that it seems everyone in my church circles tend to get really fired up about. I can't really get into deep theological conversations, nor can I get into the conversations about what the church "should be doing" outside of very basic things like receive grace and be gracious. I think about the trickier parts of Christianity, like the cross and the tomb and all the weird stories in the Old Testament, but I have a hard time focusing. I go to church because I need to. I go because where else would I go? And before you answer that for me, understand that I have pretty specific reasons why I go where I go and why I think I need to be where I am. And I think there are ways of looking at things that seem more congruent to reality than others. And I think theological issues and social issues really matter. I've picked a team, because I think it is foolish to think that you are the prophet that has figured out just the right blend that somehow everyone else has missed. But nevertheless, I probably tend to get most anxious and self-conscious about these things because people inside and outside the church tend to criticize the hell out of you or write you off as not worth listening to if your ideological Scantron doesn't contain enough of the answers on their answer key. So cut me some slack. I'm just a fellow traveler along the way, trying to make it all work and make sense.

And now, the second entryway to the actual book . . . the actual foreword.

Foreword, Proper

(Strongly Recommended)

All of this happened between the latter end of the twentieth century and the beginning of the twenty-first century. (I am not part of "Gen-X," which is, I think, a ridiculous name.) I am not in "Gen-Y" (which is, of course, even more foolish and why it is rarely used). I am not a "millennial," and while that name makes sense, I think it is foolish to suggest that a tenth-generation American kid on a farm in Kansas, an immigrant in a big city, a coastal liberal, or a middle-American standard republican WASP all share similarities because they were born during the small window of time when MTV played music videos, people didn't have e-mail addresses, and we were transitioning from tapes to CDs and VCRs to DVD players.

I am, as one sociologist suggests, part of a distinct group of people called the "Oregon Trail" generation. If you know what that means, and you didn't play this old computer game ironically or out of boredom, you are with me. We were too young to care much about Cold War politics, but we watched the first Gulf War with a kind of childish excitement and viewed the second war in the Middle East from its inception (after we watched the events of 9/11 in our dorms or first apartments). We were in our late twenties, trying to make ends meet when the banks all went to hell and the housing bubble burst. We had Facebook when you needed a .edu (or in my case, .ac.uk) suffix on your e-mail to use it, and we never dreamed that our parents would someday see the pictures we posted.

But all of this happened to us in different contexts: across spectrums of beliefs and politics, in wildly divergent places, and as folks with different races and genders.

However, references to music and pop culture should be more familiar to those from this general period. If you are reading this as an older or younger person, or in twenty years, you might need to go on the Internet to figure out some of the references.

Despite the differences in time and culture that might separate us, if there is any street value to this story, perhaps it is my attempt to take you to a place, a vantage point, from which you can observe your own monsters, recognize them as dreadful, and then press on in the peace, knowledge, and no-bullshit kind of hope that looks deep into the darkness and shrugs it off. It is a point from which the monsters are now no less real or dangerous, but like a snake charmer, you recognize the danger and can artfully handle the venomous menace.

This is no exorcism in the old-time revivalist sense. There is no "the power of Christ compels you" climactic scene to the story. This is about meeting the demons and monsters on their turf, whether in the recesses of our minds or in literal dark corners and gutters. And then, as we have allowed them to do their worst, as we have felt the madness and despair pulse through our veins, we are reminded of a hope and a peace that has overcome it all. We can then sit down on the front porch and crack a smile, maybe even laugh.

The monsters are now no less real, but they are chained, put back in their cages where they can be observed with the innocence of a child wandering past lion cages at a zoo. We ought not needlessly poke at them, and we ought not drunkenly jump into their cages. From this vantage point, everything is in its right place. Order has been restored. Despair has given way to hope.

This story is about how I discovered this vantage point, in ruinous relationships, in handcuffs, in AA meetings, and then in a peace that passes any rational understanding.

This is a story about fighting against hope . . . and losing.

CHAPTER 1

I See a Darkness

Or, Peace or Madness and Despair or Hope

A Soundtrack for Reading

1. I See a Darkness—Johnny Cash and Bonnie "Prince" Billy

2. Tonight I Shall Retire—Damien Jurado

3. Exit (Music for a Film)—Radiohead

4. Even Still—Band of Horses

5. Fort Worth Blues—Steve Earle

6. I Know It's Over—The Smiths

7. Time—Tom Waits

8. Evaporated—Ben Folds Five

9. Needle in the Hay—Elliott Smith

10. No Shade in the Shadow of the Cross—Sufjan Stevens

11. I Can't Make You Love Me—Bon Iver

12. Country Feedback—R.E.M.

Killing myself was a matter of such indifference to me that I felt like waiting for a moment when it would make some difference.

—Fyodor Dostoyevsky, "The Dream
of a Ridiculous Man"

I would pretend to have cancer. Bingo. That was it. Brilliant. All my troubles would be solved with pretend cancer and real suicide. I would say that the doctor gave me six months. No one asks for verification of cancer. That would be bad form. So no verification needed. I would look up cancer on the Internet and figure out the best kind of cancer to pretend to have. And then, after "suffering" for a little bit, I could off myself and write a letter about how death was coming and I was going to run to meet it on my terms. I would be a hero. I would be noble and strong. I was simultaneously stroking my ego and trying to soothe, once and for all, my crippling self-doubt and anxiety. I had to imagine life without me for them and then agonize over how difficult it would be. It would be a world-class narcissist move. Yet I was also feeling so crappy about myself that suicide was the only option. This wasn't a cry for help. This was a done deal.

Fake cancer would give Beth Anne (my wife) a head's up, and it would give me a few weeks to say good-bye to all the booze that I would be leaving behind.

I made this plan in the morning. By midday, I was drunk at home and figured that there were obvious holes in my plan. What if my wife wanted to talk to the doctor? What if someone had an uncle with the same cancer, and he got lesions and sores, and I was unable to reproduce these?

I overthought it. This was another stupid idea that would be impossible to execute.

So I decided to go get in my car and drive it off a bridge. That way, it would be unlikely that I would hurt anyone else. And that car was paid off. This would be especially helpful because I had no life insurance. No one has ever confronted me, timeshare-style way, to buy some. And I bought a timeshare. I would have thrown money at a death-money plan. However, I was being thoughtful of others in my suicide attempt. I have found that if you buy life insurance and then die under abnormal situations, your spouse gets locked up and charged with your death. Please note that most of my knowledge of the practical side of criminal justice comes from reruns of *Law and Order*.

As I walked down the stairs to my steel coffin, I passed the mailbox. I stopped to get the mail. It is only as I write this that it strikes me as odd that I checked the mail. What would I do with these coupons and letters? If there were an important bill, would I take it upstairs and put it on the counter? Would it follow me off the bridge to my death? What if I took it and my car blew up, action movie style, and the mail I took wasn't retrievable?

When I opened the mailbox, I found a letter addressed to me. I had recently earned my PhD, and it came with a thud. Maybe I got a pat on the back. It didn't make me want to kill myself, but I was furious about everything. Finishing college, getting married, receiving my PhD—these were supposed to be my goals. They were supposed to be end zones, places to stop, celebrate, and take a deep breath. Everything had been rushed in my adult life. But there were no end zones or final ribbons to run through.

"You did what? Congratulations. What are you up to now?"

"That's going to make things different."

"Now what?"

I don't know. I barely passed the last part of my life standing. As it turns out, things suck as much with a fancy degree as they do without one. Rain falls on all of us. We all get cavities and all eventually die.

The letter I pulled out of the mailbox was written in shaky handwriting; I recognized this as Beth Anne's grandmother's penmanship. Inside the envelope was a check for $500. What was I doing? Yeah . . . suicide. I thought, *$500 can get me something nice from the Apple Store*, and so the fatal crash and sweet release from this mortal coil would have to wait. This was 2007, and I still only had a Sony Walkman. I could get eight to twelve tracks at best with that. But now I could buy an iPod.

The ability to download and store thousands of songs did not keep me from committing suicide. But it gave one of my most serious attempts a pause. Honestly, I still have suicidal thoughts more often than I'd like. But whenever I do, I start thinking through my options, and they all sound complicated. If there were an easy suicide button, I would have checked out a while ago. Now I think I like having the idea of suicide as an option. I won't choose it, but I could, and ironically, that's enough to keep me going.

The danger of suicidal thoughts is that they seem completely rational at the time. I think this is the difference between the person contemplating self-harm and the actual ex-suicide. As I paused my exit plans to load songs and create playlists, I soon came to the realization that, while suicide seemed perfectly rational, there were other rational ideas. I went to my doctor and told him what I was planning to do. He mentioned that this was a side effect of these particular pills he prescribed. Yes, suicide was a side effect that was casually placed next to the other mundane side effects.

Warning: this medication can cause dry mouth, diarrhea, suicide, fatigue.

Really? I might gain weight too? Fuck you, Paxil.

I began a regimen of medications and medication adjustments that remains with me to the present day. Some have asked, "Why was your book delayed over and over?" The most recent reason was Zoloft. I hate that I'm a walking pharmacy with my guts and nervous system completely saturated with Klonopin, Bupropion, Lamictal, and whatever leftover business has come from at least a dozen different medications. But I'm still here. I take pills to fix my mood. I wear eyeglasses to fix my sight. I'll take advantage of modern science until I'm planted in the ground.

I was twenty-seven then. That was nearly ten years ago. Since then, I've had two children and landed a pretty good job. I'm still medicated. I still tick and still get depressed. I shake and get manic at times. But today I can wake up and laugh. I had the option of being dead. I do what I do because I had the option not to. I'm what's called an ex-suicide.

This story, and the various stories that compose the main narrative, involve a long and winding road of dark, cringe-inducing, and possibly humorous stories about how I learned to live with madness and despair and learn that hope, while dangerous in its own way, is the antidote and the key that keeps my monsters in their cages.

Hope

Most quotes about hope are bullshit. They sound more like wishing than hoping. We confuse hope with dreaming or wanting to catch a break. We hope it doesn't rain. We hope to get out of jury duty. We hope to be successful later in life. I need real hope. The kind of hope that is pining for something so inexpressibly beautiful that it crushes you, since you know you might not get it, and you fear that the weight of the thing might crush you as well. Wishing and dreaming are soft middle-class substitutes. Hope is harder to pin down. Hope is a wily bastard.

I remember vividly (which is rare for so many things during a decade or so of my life) when I heard the line from *The Shawshank Redemption*: "Hope is a dangerous thing. Hope can drive a man insane." Red, the character played by Morgan Freeman, goes on to extol hope, but not the kind found in the Hallmark cards. His hope is real and dangerous and somehow too good to be true. I need hope to be like that, in that Morgan Freeman voiceover that makes everything sound ten times more important.

I can't take the kind of hope peddled by TV preachers with shiny teeth and shiny hair.

They proclaim, in the anti-Freeman voice of Joel Osteen,

Hope!
Dream!
Have faith!

Stop. Please. While you're perched upon your happy hills of enchantment, some of us are dying down here. Dying down here in the swamp of despair and doubt and self-destruction.

My story is one of "hoping against hope." That could mean something like "hoping really hard," but when I first heard the phrase, I took it to be an oxymoron or like a Zen koan. Yet hoping against hope is realizing that we've got nothing, though we are searching for something. But that something is so great and powerful and heavy that we might not want it. Hope is crushing and dangerous. Hope is different from wishing. I can wish like a bastard. I can wish to my heart's content. Wishing is a penny in the fountain or a quick look to the sky. I can wish for a million bucks. Wishing, as I see it, is being open to something happening to you that removes some of the crap you've built up for yourself. Hope, on the other hand, is concrete. It doesn't win a scratcher or let the fumbled ball bounce into the hands of a guy on your team. Hope kills death. Hope kills despair. Hope sets things right. And the more I think that can't happen, the more futile and dangerous I think hope is. But everything is going to be OK. We hope.

But instead of ending this story with a "happily ever after," I prefer to borrow a line from the end of *The Great Gatsby*: "So we beat on, boats against the current, borne back ceaselessly into the past."

I have been beaten back throughout the time it took to write this book. I've been trying to pin down a moving person: me. I want to put myself up on a corkboard with pins like a butterfly. But as I write, life keeps happening. And I am continually pushed back by the tides of life. But I have hope it will not always be like this, even when I want to fight against hope or when I am sure I am hoping for lost causes.

I bet against hope. I railed against hope. I hoped against hope. And I lost. Hope won out. I've been fighting it for years now, and I'm afraid some type of hope has me licked. But still, it isn't the bullshit kind you find in Internet memes. I will explain by considering hope's opposite.

Hope is the opposite of despair. Or, as the medieval church called it: sloth. Based on that one scene in the movie *Se7en*, with Brad Pitt, I figured sloth was not getting to the gym enough. But sloth, a form of cosmic despair, is way worse. It is giving up. It is admitting that everything is merely sound and fury, signifying nothing.

We talk flippantly about things like hopelessness or despair or lost causes, when things aren't going our way, when we are seven games back with a week to go in the season, or when we are down ten points with thirty seconds to go. We might think of hopelessness as a feeling we get when no one is hiring or when she isn't calling back. But I think these are just garden-variety bummers. Real bummers of course, but more a "damn it" than a "time to start reading up on how the car in the closed garage with the running motor thing works." Granted, little things can start as bummers and then grow and wrap themselves around us with their dark tentacles and cause us to truly despair.

Sloth is thinking, "nothing good can happen, and so I'm just going to stop working toward anything." It's not about being lazy; it's about trying to kick through a steel door and then just giving up. You tried. It just didn't work.

But maybe hope is impossible to shake, because somewhere along the line we realize that despair can only be temporal. It has a shelf life. Despair can only really be despair if we know what's written on the last page. We have to know the end of the story to know that it is hopeless. And as long as that last page isn't written, there's a crack of light.

That is hope.

You don't have to believe in it for it to be there. It just is. I had to get used to this, and I am still often uncomfortable knowing that it is. It's my default setting.

At some point, we learn to live on these settings like we are on autopilot. We enter our coordinates, and barring major setbacks, we get to our destination. In high school, super perky Justine was on an autopilot course that coasted her into Harvard and then some swanky law firm.[1] Or maybe it was like trying-hard-to-be-tough Brian, whose upbringing and autopilot settings had him eventually transfer to the "experimental" high school, have a few kids with different women, and end up working a couple of menial jobs to pay child support before he took off for a no-questions-asked job doing hard labor in Alaska.

Maybe your autopilot settings are coded into your DNA, or formed by your parents, or the television you watch between the ages of four and eight. My autopilot settings might not have been on full despair mode as a kid, but they were somewhere between "someone else can do it better" and "it probably won't work out." As a kid, you can deal with this by lashing out or getting into sad British pop. As a teenager, it starts to fester and can grow into something benign, like maybe, "I'm cool hanging out around here, hitting the junior college

---

[1] There are rumors that because she's Mormon, she probably works for the CIA now. It's how the CIA works. They like Mormons. Mormons are super nice and have clean records and maybe have a little bit of a mean streak in them that lets them do some of the secret dirty work.

circuit, and then working in sales." Or it starts to whip into a frenzy, eventually releasing itself as despair in the sense of complete hopelessness, chaos, and madness.

My narrative might have different twists and turns than yours. Your story probably has different prescriptions and temporary solutions. But the metanarrative for all of us, as it seems to me, is the cosmic battle between hope and despair and between peace and madness.

I've seen the bottom, and I've started to think there is a crack of light—something written on that last page—the feeling that if I am done for, lost, and hopeless (feelings I still have from time to time), there is a cosmic truth and a deep magic that only allow despair to be temporal.

CHAPTER 2

Making the Skeletons Dance

Or, Rumors and Unsubstantiated Stories about My Family Tree

A Soundtrack for Reading

1. Blue in Green—Miles Davis
2. Blue Skies—Art Tatum
3. Autumn Leaves—Chet Baker
4. Desafinado—Stan Getz and Charlie Byrd
5. Ruby, My Dear—Thelonious Monk
6. I'm Old Fashioned—John Coltrane
7. Alice in Wonderland—Dave Brubeck and Paul Desmond
8. Somewhere over the Rainbow—Paul Gonsalves
9. In a Sentimental Mood—Duke Ellington
10. My Blue Heaven—Jo Jones
11. Blue Rondo a la Turk—Dave Brubeck
12. Desafinado—Dizzy Gillespie

If you cannot get rid of the family skeleton, you may as well make it dance.

—George Bernard Shaw

I'm going to start this with prehistory. Stuff that came before me is hard to confirm with absolute certainty, but it shaped the way I came into the world nonetheless. The stories are almost all true. Even if some are not completely true, the way in which they came down to us helped us create a family narrative and try to make sense of a particularly chaotic family.

I've told people stories about my family before. In small doses, they haven't seemed that peculiar, but I guess putting them all together makes for a story worth telling. At least two of my great grandparents had connections to the mob, three of my grandparents were alcoholics, and at least one committed suicide. Shiftiness, nerves, the desire for substances, and dancing close to the line of illegality were things etched into my DNA.

I don't want to try to make up stuff about my family that isn't true. I have spent time trying to plumb the depths of the strange family stories that always swirled about in whispers. I don't have everything down perfectly, but I've been able to get the main characters and the bullet points of their lives in such an order that I can tell the story, with a few unsubstantiated claims, in fairly good detail. And holy crap, it's a good story.

I'll start with my mom's side.

The MacIntyres

The MacIntyres were Scottish and Native American, so you might guess that being prone to hitting the bottle heavy wasn't a shock. I don't mean to get stereotypical, but Scots and Native Americans are known for their fondness for the drink, but then again, it seems that all people who talk about their ancestors mention their propensity to drink. What culture doesn't make that claim? The Dutch. These are my people. We've not got a reputation for being big drinkers. We're famous for double Dutch chocolate, double Dutch jump rope, and the idea that both participants in a date should pay. We also have windmills and wooden shoes. Of any cultural footwear, I suppose none would be less conducive to a night out drinking than the wooden variety. But the MacIntyres were a mystery, pickled by alcohol and smelling, faintly, of lost opportunities, questionable financial decisions, and untimely deaths.

The MacIntyres lived in San Francisco at the turn of the century. Some died when their house collapsed during the great earthquake of 1906. My great-great-grandmother was on the bottom floor, and when the top floor collapsed, her mother was impaled on something and lay next to her bleeding out as my great-great-grandmother sat in shock, watching her die. These are the types of stories that have been passed down. I bet some of them saw Honus Wagner play baseball and played on the trolley cars and had lavish parties and exotic vacations. But we don't tell those stories in this family. This family revels in the morbid. All the old family pictures make them look like the Addams Family. They are staring dead-eyed just beyond the camera. They were straight-collared with hard jawlines and hair carefully slicked or pulled back. The biggest of the brothers played football at Stanford, old-timey style, with leather helmets. He died from a collision on the field. Another of his sisters was severely mentally disabled (born with a deformed head, possibly damaged by forceps at birth) and was quietly put in a nunnery. The family was religious and well-off; they were major donors to a Catholic college in California and have a dormitory and a few other things named after them. Outside of the buildings at the college, the brother that died playing football, and the mentally impaired nun, we don't know much about the rest, except for the twins: Harold and William.

Harold was my grandpa. He is something of a mythical figure in my family, at least insofar as I remember the one picture we had of him as an adult. He was a giant, dark leather-faced man, with giant hands and a giant brush of jet black hair—looking more Cherokee than Scottish. He went by Hal, a bitchin' nickname for someone called Harold. He looked neither intimidating nor particularly kind. He squinted into the camera, which was below his line of sight, and he had his giant paw around my waif-like, thickly bespectacled grandma. He was a twin, one of the last two of a family of ten. His dad was a cop in San Francisco and apparently rose through the ranks pretty quickly, making lieutenant by 1920. He made his money on the force, but also for working with the mob during prohibition. Eventually, he was caught and fired. Luckily, his wife would spend her days taking some of the ill-gotten cash down to the city center and playing the stock market. She was fond of a little company called General Electric and decided to invest in it. While everyone else was living Steinbeck-style during the depression, they lived in luxury and retired young on the coast near San Francisco. My great-grandfather died (reportedly mob related) and left his now fabulously wealthy wife a widow. She lived to an old enough age to see one of her young-est sons (my grandpa) die. He died from some combination of booze, cancer, and a mysterious experimental surgery in Mexico (a trio that will probably always lead to an untimely death). As his mother was not yet dead, he hadn't received his inheritance and had his brother swear that he would give him Viola Harold's share. Except Viola was hated by the family, since she was kind of creepy, angry, and a Catholic. People of Scottish and Cherokee descent are virulently anti-Catholic, or so I am led to believe, if they are staunch Jacobites and were displaced by the followers of Father Junipero de Serra and the first Jesuit missionaries on the West Coast.

William took the money and ran. By the time I was born, my grandma was living on the dole in that crappy small house in Riverside. William was the Elijah Wood to Harold's Macaulay Culkin. This is a reference to the underrated *The Good Son*. Culkin wanted to play against type and became my go-to reference for the bad one in any pair. I currently have a pair of shoes and one of them is messed up. It was Culkined. "The Culkin one" would be my response if I lost that one and was asked which of the two I couldn't find. My grandpa was Culkined.

Harold married a Scottish woman named Viola Bernice. He kept it in the clan. She was from Nevada. She is less of a mystery to me perhaps because she was the only grandparent that was alive when I was born. We called her "Nana," which confused me, because that was the name of the dog in the cartoon version of *Peter Pan*. Her house smelled like cigarettes, and she always had *Smurfs* coloring books for us and baseball games on the TV. She wore a funny rag on her head and glasses so thick you couldn't see her eyes. I remember being scared of her. She died when I was four. I remember being told that she had died. I was looking at a poster with planets on it. I've always stared at pictures of space because I think it would be interesting to learn more. However, like Ireland, it will remain a place I know little about because I'm busy. From the age of four, I looked at things to show that I was distracted and probably didn't want to be there. People cried and spoke in hushed tones about her. I remember thinking that wherever she was, it was probably better than the shit hole she lived in. I wasn't upset by the whole thing, and I don't blame myself for not being that affected by the death of a kind of creepy old woman with eyes you couldn't see and a discernable stench that emanated from her and filled the house.

When we went to visit my grandma, I remember wanting to go down to the house that belonged to a woman we called "Aunt Sandy," a friend of my grandma's. Aunt Sandy was not a blood relative, but she let us watch television and eat whatever junk food she had. She was the closest thing I had to a grandparent growing up, and she was a widowed woman in a depressing cul-de-sac for forgotten widows and let us eat packaged cookies and watch movies about race cars and orphans. (At least the one I remember watching multiple times was about these things. I believe it was called *Six Pack* and starred Kenny Rogers.) She too loved baseball. When I played on my first team, the Tigers of St. Margaret's Church, Aunt Sandy came to all the games. We made the playoffs and eventually went to the championship game against a team from across town with primarily Latino kids that looked ten years older than us. The game was a disaster, and as they were in the process of destroying us, we all heard the crash.

She was a very large woman, maybe just shy of four hundred pounds. She was sitting on a beach chair right behind us in the dugout. She tried to get up but had a massive heart attack, fell back on her chair, broke it, and fell to the ground. A giant elderly dead woman in a muumuu lying on the concrete next to a broken chair, and a dozen seven-year-olds looking on in horror. The game was delayed by the paramedics, and I remember they needed help from parents getting her onto a gurney to put in the ambulance. We lost because the other team was far superior. But we blamed Aunt Sandy's untimely and morbidly curious death. I'm sure there were happier stories, but being part MacIntyre, I have learned to tell the sad and morbid ones.

The van Voorhis Clan

The van Voorhis family came to America in the seventeenth and eighteenth centuries.[1] The family name is tied to a farm in the Netherlands, and so we can say with a good bit of certainty that we've all got the same blood in our veins. Most of the family came to upstate New York, a place called Fishkill. Some moved south to West Virginia and others to Ohio. These are the main centers of van Voorhis family history. The family is tied to several episodes within American history. A Captain Daniel van Voorhis shipped supplies between the colonies and the Netherlands during the War of Independence. He was stopped twice with a warning (apparently, he had more than baked goods and cider on board). The third time he was caught, he was unceremoniously hung aboard his own ship. Another Daniel van Voorhis was a silversmith who has a number of pieces in museums across America. I saw one once. I don't know much about silversmithing; it was never that impressive to me, but I guess it is decent enough for the Smithsonian. Cornelius Westbrook van Voorhis was the original host of the *Twilight Zone* until head writer and director Rod Serling decided he could do a better job. Cornelius made his dollars as the voice of the premovie newsreels in the '40s scaring the hell out of people about the Nazi scourge rising in the Old Country.

Bruce van Voorhis won a Medal of Honor posthumously after being shot down in the Pacific theater during World War II. Bruce had a destroyer named after him, and a naval squadron is still named after him.

Another Daniel van Voorhis, from my direct family line in Zanesville, Ohio, was called the "Father of Modern Tank Warfare" as the commander of the Army's first "mechanized" cavalry; he was a lieutenant general and fought in the Spanish American War and both World Wars.

And somehow, this august family (which also included a number of circuit-riding pastors on the western front in the Ohio River

---

[1] van Voorhis, with the lower case *v*, was something I started doing to my name in my twenties. It was a traditional spelling, and I wanted to identify and distinguish my family line from the Van Voorhis family in California, which seems to be an unfortunate oddity in an otherwise distinguished family tree. Also, the spelling is Voorhees, Vorhis, Vanvoorhees, and a few more. It doesn't matter, no one will ever pronounce it properly.

valley) spat out my grandfather. His name was Ross Parker, which I thought would be a good name for a son, until my wife reminded me that he was a world-class asshole.

Ross left his family behind in Ohio to try his luck in California. He didn't dig the family's religious inclinations, and apparently, they weren't big fans of his hard drinking, womanizing, or poor money management. He left Zanesville for Los Angeles with a friend, and the two of them had the idea that they could make money on the ponies because, you know, professional horse bettors are notoriously and fabulously wealthy. At some point, he met a woman on a trolley named Ann. She came from a wealthy family. So of course, it must have been love at Ross's first sight. They cranked out seven kids. Ann started to go blind when the oldest (my aunt) was still young. Ross worked in coal, or oil, or something that made him come home covered in soot, wearing oil-stained coveralls and smelling like booze. Meanwhile, Ann was mentally unstable or, as they called it back then, someone who "had the worries." She wouldn't let any of the children call her "Mom," only "Ann," but I don't think in the cute and homey way Scout called her dad Atticus. Ann didn't deal well with the lousy husband or the kids. At some point in her life, when my oldest aunt was young, Ann chased her around the kitchen with a carving knife, which, as a legally blind lady, is a terrible idea. After having her last kid (my old man), she had had enough. I can only imagine the dread of having seven kids, a lousy drunk of a husband, very little money, and being blind. She killed herself somewhere near the end of the 1930s. My own dad would have been quite young, and his older siblings had gotten married and moved out on their own. My dad only had his father, Ross, and they lived together for a while, in a makeshift studio in someone's garage. My dad would be at home some nights waiting for dinner and eventually walk out in the Raymond Carver–esque streets of 1940s Los Angeles, going from bar to bar looking for his father. Eventually, Ross decided he couldn't watch his boy anymore, so he dropped him off at an orphanage. Why didn't any of my dad's brothers or sisters take him in? I met a few of them: they were a lousy bunch as well, except Dirk, who had giant worn hands and a warm smile, looked like Chuck Yeager, and flew planes . . . and his name was Dirk (you can't pull that name off without being a badass). My grandpa would occasionally come visit my dad. What kind of strange open orphanage does this? Perhaps it was more like a daycare where he left his kid during long benders. The last time he saw my dad, he gave him a turtle and walked away.

Ross died from the drink sometime in the late 1940s, thirty years before I was born. My dad never ended up getting adopted, so he eventually left Los Angeles at eighteen. He met a lady when he had to drive his friend up to San Francisco to meet his friend's girlfriend, because a broken leg prevented his buddy from driving. My dad's friend's girlfriend had a younger sister, who he eventually married at some point and, rumor has it, had a few kids, of which I am the youngest.

CHAPTER 3

The Boy with the Thorn in His Side

Or, Growing Up with Power Ballads and TV Shows with Strangely Functional Families

A Soundtrack for Reading

1. The Boy with the Thorn in His Side—The Smiths
2. Good Thing—Fine Young Cannibals
3. Don't Lose My Number—Phil Collins
4. Never Gonna Give You Up—Rick Astley
5. Everlasting Love—Howard Jones
6. Brothers in Arms—Dire Straits
7. Heaven Can Wait—Meat Loaf
8. Total Eclipse of the Heart—Bonnie Tyler
9. Heaven—Bryan Adams
10. Right Here Waiting—Richard Marx
11. Arthur's Theme—Christopher Cross
12. Come Sail Away—Styx

*Anybody who has survived his childhood has enough
information about life to last him the rest of his days.*

—Flannery O'Connor

My mother died while giving birth to me. She was an older mother, and I was an accident. When I decided to make my world debut in February 1979, I didn't know that the mountain home we had recently moved into was too remote for ambulances. It snowed, my parents were caught in the weather, and I was born and killed my mom. This is the extent of the narrative. The only thing worse than killing your mother at childbirth is not *technically* killing her and being blamed for it, despite her not actually dying. (I was a difficult delivery and she flatlined for a few seconds.) According to her story, she died but returned to earth when an angel asked her if she would rather live in heaven or back at home (I have no idea why she would pick a lower middle-class existence over paradise). But she liked to emphasize the killing and dying part. The worst part of it was being reminded, ad nauseam, that I killed her as she reveled in telling friends and family.

I had to live with the guilt of it for many years growing up. I had no choice, as my mother would remind me whenever possible.

Sometime in the mid-1970s, my parents decided to leave the Southern California suburbs for a mountain home about an hour's drive away. (I have no idea how far it really was, since in Southern California, we measure distance by drive time. A mile only makes sense when it's contextualized and adjusted for location and time of day.) It was possibly some kind of charity or agreement with the Catholic Church, which owned the property and for which my mom was going to run a daycare. I can only make sense of this move if I understand our radical relocation as fiscally driven by charity or a quid pro quo agreement with the church. The house was still being finished, or maybe it was getting remodeled. It's hard to know, since we didn't have build-a-custom-house kind of money. Living in a half-finished house fits Adam Carolla's theory that rich people and poor people share similarities that the middle class will never know. Living in a house that is halfway finished could mean that you are rich and have constant remodels, like when you're adding a wing.

Poor people, on the other hand, might have a house they couldn't afford to finish or live in a dwelling being built for them by a charity. Or maybe it is a good squatting opportunity, as the workers on-site have predictable times of arriving and leaving. On-site one day, as the house was being worked on, my sister and I thought it would be funny to take turns running up and down the stairs to the wall-sized open window cavity that was on the second floor. From that perch, we would wave down to each other. After doing this a few times, my waving became overly zealous, and I fell out of the gaping hole where the glass should have been. I've been told that my parents saw me falling from across the property, and they held their breath. I don't doubt that story, but it still seems odd. You'd have to be watching me intently to catch that quick of a fall. I'm not calling them liars; it's just that I would have been shouting at my son to get the hell down from a gaping hole in the second story of our home. Nevertheless, everyone came running to me, and I jumped up like a magician having performed his grand finale. At least this is what I remember. But it has been told to me so many times, it might be my fabricated image of what it looked like that has now been implanted as the actual memory. Nevertheless, I suppose I could have died early and erased years of addiction and sorrow, but I had a few more decades left to wander this rock floating in space. Maybe I was granted a chance to try to make sense of all the madness and then write it down for you, dear reader.

My memories—implanted or otherwise—are almost all bleak. I killed my mother at childbirth, I scared everyone through an almost gruesome and untimely death, and I can also remember the first time I tried running away from home. The idea of running away and living on trains like the kids in the *Boxcar Children* books, or the Disney Channel original *The Journey of Natty Gann*, seemed like bliss. I imagined that I would end up in an orphanage where I could be left alone or get picked up by a family like the Seavers on *Growing Pains*, who adopted a young Leonardo DiCaprio near the end of the show's run. Or maybe it would be finding something like a boarding house for boys like the one run by Mrs. Garrett on the *Facts of Life*. Nevertheless, I was under five and already thinking that any kind of alternate life would be better.

I never became an orphan, technically, and we moved back down the mountain when I was about five. I remember wetting my bed well past the age of respectability, and my mom threatened to put me back into diapers. I remember watching the 1984 Olympics with the Soviet Union boycotting, Mary Lou Retton's perfect ten, and Mary Decker Slaney falling into a heap on the ground at the beginning of the race and her terrifying and heartbreaking sobs. My earliest memories, and many memories since, can be tracked down by placing them near specific years when the Olympics took place. I find this interesting because, first, I have an unhealthy love of the Summer Olympics. Second, it seems that my parents had an analogous relationship with me. Every four years or so, they would get into what I was doing in the same way I might get into watching indoor cycling. Thus my parents would become interested in me for semi-intense spurts of time but with long breaks in between.[1]

The dominant, palpable emotion from those early years was fear. Fear of spilling something under the glass on the wooden table. Fear of getting electrocuted, of earthquakes, and of killer bees. We had a free magazine at school called *The Weekly Reader*, and it would regale us with stories designed to make us feel bad. ("Guess What These Poor Kids Don't Have?" may have been a title of a story, and "We Are All Going to Be Killed by Bees or Earthquakes" could have been another.) But I was also afraid of nonnatural disasters. I was afraid of being made fun of and not learning how to do things that other kids could do like ride a bike, throw a baseball, or avoid urinating on myself. I was also afraid of fast things, bright things, and loud things. I know now that I have hypervigilance—the curse of being more aware of my surroundings than needed. It's helpful when I get bored and want to listen in on others' conversations or when I am walking down dark alleys at night. But it's more annoying when you have to live with a family that chews everything ten times more loudly than

---

[1] What's most sad about this is that I wrote this after the China Olympics and before the Rio Olympics. The Rio Olympics seemed like the end of an era. No spoiler alerts, no national frenzy over a record or new national "sweetheart." The Olympics seem like some families' Thanksgivings; they still happen, but there is no real pomp or circumstance or effort. It's like everyone is kind of doing it because they are supposed to. But no one cares as much as they used to. And yams with marshmallows = Olympic Men's Basketball (ask me in person about this one).

average humans. I would eat with my elbows on the table and hands cupped over my ears, and for this, I'd be yelled at and spend the rest of the meal in excruciating discomfort as soup was slurped and milk gulped. I would go to the table with fear. I remember being yelled at and then having to sit in unbearable silence. I would try to wear a sweatshirt with a hood or start conversations to keep people from putting food in their mouths. I lived in fear of the kitchen table, the telephone that I was always certain had juvenile correction officers on the other side, and public bathrooms. Eating, the phone ringing, and having to go to the bathroom in public still make me uncomfortable. My medication takes care of some of this today, but if I am stressed and you are going to eat anything in front of me, don't take offense if I excuse myself to pop a Klonopin. Nonetheless, I still can overthink these situations and start to breathe heavily, repeat words over and over, hit the sides of my legs, blink excessively, and twitch.

As early as the second grade, I was acutely aware that some people were good and others were bad. I only thought in binary terms. But I should have realized from experience that this wasn't the case. Some people are just ghosts, neither particularly good nor bad: they just exist. They don't matter at all. Not mattering is my greatest fear today; it was then too. I wasn't old enough to have existential dread about the cosmos or the nature of healthy relationships and mutual affirmation. All I knew was that I walked around unsure of what might happen and what I was supposed to do. I was afraid of having to be homeless. I was afraid that people were talking about me behind my back. I was afraid I was doing it all wrong. Fears that might be semirational based on circumstances for adults were my biggest fears around the age of seven.[2]

---

[2] This book, you will notice, has very little to say about my parents. This is intentional, and partly because I have moved beyond any notion of "childhood trauma" as the root of my insecurities. They certainly did do loving things for me, but my fear of them and my overwhelming discomfort in reminiscing about my childhood have caused me to block out most of our interactions. If they wrote their own books or would have written in this book, they might defend themselves as busy, ill, or working too hard. I have moved on and accept responsibility for my own actions, even those that were conditioned by my family's histories. As I have grown older and compared stories about growing up, I'm often met with shock from friends who hear stories about the way I was raised. Part of this has to do with my own initiative to get outside the house and spend as much time by myself as possible. Maybe I should have asked them to tell me they loved me or taken the initiative and said it myself.

*   *   *

One of my favorite distractions from irrational fears was a small brown radio that I placed next to my pillow, on my mattress, on the ground. It was so old it didn't have a clock, and only the AM band had numbers. You had to know where your FM stations were in relation to the AM station numbers if you wanted to find them. Also, it started to smell like burning plastic if I left it on too long.

From the age of five on, this fear was usually overcome by euphoria I got from my professional sports teams: the Angels, Rams, and Clippers. Being a fan of any of these franchises in the '80s was enough to suggest I was in a gloomy state. They were losers like me. They all had their successful crosstown rivals (Dodgers, Raiders, Lakers). My quixotic love for them arose from a sensitive emotionalism that pined for at least some kind of relationship, particularly the kind I imagined was behind the ballads on the adult contemporary stations. Kirk McCaskill, the Canadian pitcher on the Angels with a mullet, and Richard Marx, the American balladeer with a prodigious mullet, became two people upon whose fate my moods would rise or fall.

I can see now that I had what my grandmother's generation called "the worries" from an early age. I was scared to find friends, use public toilets, and walk past boys my age for fear of being talked to or beaten to a pulp. I was scared of sticking out but also afraid of blending in and becoming one of those kids I was secretly afraid of being: normal, adjusted, and seemingly just OK. I certainly didn't know that I had a severe anxiety disorder or bouts of deep depression and self-loathing, but it all makes sense looking back. It had to be something; I just wasn't sure what. And so I ventured out into the neighborhood from time to time, but usually with disastrous results.

M***********

I sort of made friends when we moved into a new house. I was still five. Two brothers lived across the street; the youngest of the pair

---

I don't doubt their parental affection for their own offspring—that's biological—plus, if you aren't drowned by your mother in a bathtub during a bout of postpartum depression or shot by your dad in a heated argument (like Marvin Gaye), there was likely enough affection to get you through life.

would eat food off the ground if his brother told him to, and the other, to this day, goes by Peter-the-weird-kid-who-was-way-too-into-trains.

I was generally inactive for fear of getting hurt and resisted anything that might cause my heart rate to rise. I tend to remember conversations and how things felt. Maybe because of this, I can still feel the grass under my feet when I felt one of my earliest bursts of excitement, shame, and shock.

I was called a motherfucker.

And by Peter-the-weird-kid-who-was-way-too-into-trains, of all people.

The neighborhood kids and I were using words like "nerd" and "dork." Sometimes we tried to shoehorn in a "damn" here and there. But those words were like popguns compared to Peter's use of the nuclear option: motherfucker. I didn't even know what it meant. I could do the noun + verb math, but the mere sound of the phrase was simultaneously euphonious and vicious. It sounded like a freight train coming out of his mouth, heading my way.

I should recall for you the offending behavior that led to this momentous event.

I thought it would be a good idea to open a bike repair shop. Not really a shop, but a front lawn with a lousy sign I made with a marker. The other kids had lemonade stands. It was usually that powdered shit too. And the money they made was usually from benefactors (their parents or kindly strangers in passing cars). But my not-yet-fully-formed cerebral cortex had figured something out about the free market and children: we could do without lemonade; we could not do without our bikes.

Somehow I got ahold of my dad's tools, probably only a wrench and a screwdriver (he wasn't very handy). I then convinced the other children on the street that, despite their bikes working fine as they passed me, they needed repairs.

Cut to later that evening.

I was standing in my yard with bits of metal and plastic strewn about. I hadn't collected any money. Did I know what to charge relative to the lemonade economy? I wish I remembered. Peter, Ryan, Jamie, the red-haired-kid-who-lived-in-the-house-where-a-guy-hung-himself-in-the-garage, the kid-whose-yard-had-a-car-on-blocks-and-a-house-that-smelled-like-cat-piss-but-we-put-up-with-him-because-he-had-a-Nintendo, and a few others came to my yard. My first crush, Jamie, laughed. Her brother Ryan was confused. I don't remember much of the conversations we had while standing over the dissected bicycles, but I remember being afraid. I thought someone would punch me. Or tell the others not to play with me anymore. I hoped that they would "tell on me." That would be the best outcome, since my parents wouldn't do anything. But I remember the fear. I remember that tinfoil taste in the back of my mouth.

I think we all stood around, not quite sure what to make of the strange, erratic thing I had done. I was terrified, and they were probably curious as to how they would tell their parents that they gave a kid with a couple tools their perfectly functioning bikes to "fix."

And then, standing around in dumbfounded silence, it happened. Peter called me a motherfucker. Bingo, it was the perfect response. It sounded brutal and round and harsh but euphonious. It jolted us all back to reality. What I did with the bikes was unfortunate but not morally dubious. Peter said the word we all knew meant immediate dismissal and would generate fodder for neighborhood gossip. For me, it was also liberating; there was nothing below that word, nothing you could be called that was worse. I'd taken the strongest punch possible and was still standing. It was a brilliant gift in the disguise of an insult; those were the four most brilliantly configured syllables in the English language. Even if it had no inflammatory or creepy incestuous innuendo, it would still come from pursed lips and then off your tongue and between your top teeth and bottom lip like a bolt from the heavens.

Someone—I think it was Jamie—said she was going to tell on him; but Peter insisted he had only said the name of the hamburger chain Fuddruckers. He had plausible deniability at least. Happily, the shock of the dropping of the worst cognate of the F-bomb temporarily stunned the neighborhood kids and kept them from being angry at me about their dismembered bikes. Eventually, someone's dad and older sibling came out to reassemble the bikes.

Trying to fix other kids' bikes was the kind of foolish thing I did to try to get validation but unfortunately received scorn for doing. I should note that I was available to fix them instead of ride around with them because I didn't actually own a bike. In shame, I slowly retreated from kids my age and into my room and spent my free time there for the next few years. Occasionally, I would meet someone at school and be invited into his house, but being terrified that he would have to then come to my house too, I usually turned down the invitations, except one time when a boy called Greg invited me to his house to play computer games. His brother threw up on me in the car, and having no change of clothes, I sat around with vomit on my shirt and pants while I ate a cheeseburger from McDonalds. I watched as Greg spent the majority of the time playing the games he told me I wouldn't know how to play.

Gifted, Talented, and Unable to Hold It In

I spent as much time as I could with teachers. They were safer, I thought. I had a curious number of male teachers, most of whom may have seen a broken kid and decided that they should let me hang out in the classroom during breaks. My general lack of sociability, and also getting embarrassed by my poor soccer and handball skills, made me leery of the playground.

Also, there were rumors of being pushed into the bathroom during physical education classes. I have no idea why I thought someone would force me to walk into the boy's bathroom. But it scared the hell out of me.

My fear, now just a general discomfort, of public restrooms can be traced back to the second grade. This was the first year I went to school, not because I was gifted or homeschooled, but because my parents weren't the proactive sort.

In the second grade some of the kids played a game called "fireman" in the bathroom. Apparently, they would pee in the urinal and then start backing up and see how far they could manage to keep their stream hitting the bowl. And if you lost, everyone got to take turns flicking your penis with their fingers. I was so terrified to urinate (or worse, defecate) on school grounds that I monitored my water and food intake while at school and ran home after class every day to use the toilet and microwave a hot dog for myself. If I missed the light by the Stop N' Go, or we were held late by the teacher, I went into DEFCON 1 mode.

One day, I sat cross-legged on the ground, listening to our teacher, a Kramer lookalike who practiced Buddhism, tell us the story of Don Quixote. I can remember him singing part of "The Impossible Dream" from the musical version of Cervantes novel. I could feel the sensation of having to pee come upon me. I also remember thinking that, if I gulped air in through my mouth and nose, perhaps the pee would ascend back up into my bladder. And then I slowly felt the thin, grade-school carpet warm around me. As others started to sniff and look around, the tall curly haired man broke from the verse he was singing and told me to go to the front office. I left a wet circle on the cheap carpet, now wearing wet Levi's. For some reason, I decided that I couldn't go into the office, so I hid behind the bushes. A teacher saw me there and insisted that I go into the office so my parents could bring me a new pair of pants. I obliged and sat on the nurse's examining table, perched on a towel for the rest of the day. When school ended and my parents had not come with a pair of new pants, I raced home, bolted into my room, and changed. As slyly as possible, I took the wet jeans and threw them over the back fence into an adjacent parking lot.

After that, not many of the second or third graders at Magnolia Elementary would invite me to their birthday parties or let me join their soccer games. I spent most of these early years in school being quiet, short, and anxious. I missed a lot of school because my mom told me I didn't have to go if I didn't want to. This is still baffling to me, and it led to enough truancy that I spent a good part of high school in Saturday school and failed to make the grades to be accepted into any college. I also changed schools every two years, so I never had any lasting friendships. I was also handicapped in the friend-making department in that, at some point, a teacher requested to have me tested for the "gifted" (GATE) classes. I remember sitting in the district office, doing puzzles and math. I also remember when I was told that I would be entering into GATE classes, I asked my Dad how I did on the test. He told me, "I'd tell you, but I don't want your head getting too big." In any case, this put me in the room of misfit boys and girls, usually foreign kids with parents who took an active role in their children's education. I had no such luck on either account. Even these kids rejected me, since I didn't like to read, and I wasn't interested in any subject that didn't involve sports or pop music.

The Junior Olympics

Despite my love of sports, and eventually becoming a decent baseball player, I was possibly the least athletic kid in school. Or at best, I was the least athletic kid who wanted to be athletic. My lack of athletic ability may have been due to my short stature (I didn't break five feet until I reached sixth grade) or my physique, which relegated me to finding the jeans for boys labeled "husky." Do they still do this? At least when I was 250 pounds, I could just look for the number forty for the waist; there was no "jumbo" or "chunky" version of large pants to remind you of your bulbous shape. But there was a secret behind my strange performance in sports that I couldn't reveal: I didn't know how to tie my shoes until I was in the fourth grade. I could have kept wearing Velcro shoes, but my shoes were always off brand and embarrassing enough. At least lace-ups could look somewhat athletic, though, only if they were properly laced and tied. It was like *Sophie's Choice* but with a nine-year-old child's choice of footwear. The choice I made led to one of the most embarrassing moments of my preteen life.

I'm not sure how I entered the Junior Olympics. I don't know if it was something everyone in second grade did or if I went out of my way to sign up for it. For the sake of organization, they had everyone register for two different events. I signed up for the high jump, which should have been the last thing a short stump of a kid should attempt. But I had recently read about Dick Fosbury, and I figured I could use his technique to beat all the other kids in my age bracket. I had visions of being lifted up on the shoulders of Mike Martinez, Brandon Foster, and other third grade luminaries, to the cheering of the girls who wouldn't otherwise acknowledge me. The problem was, I had to sign up for another event. I remember making the argument—this on the heels of the Seoul Olympics—that it would be ridiculous to force an athlete to sign up for more than one event. You only had to know one sport in life, I argued to no avail. I signed up to run the half-mile. Having the "half" in it made it sound less daunting. But the high jump came afterward, so, I reasoned, my high jumping fame could erase any memories of my lack of coordination, endurance, or speed.

I remember bolting off the line at the whistle. I almost immediately felt a sting in my side and started to feel like my esophagus was being squeezed. My face was turning beet red. I slowed but kept going. As I started down the last leg of the first lap, I realized a few things. One, I was far behind everyone else. Two, the other boys kept running despite finishing the first lap. Apparently, a half-mile is two times around the track. And three, my shoelaces were coming undone. I struggled to decide which would bring more shame: losing with shoes untied, or losing really badly with shoes somewhat tied. Or, I could walk off the track. As a chubby second grader with few friends and an acute self-consciousness, the options paralyzed me. I slowed to a jog and tried reaching down to tuck my shoelaces into the sides of my off-brand running shoes. My jog began to look like a kind of skipping, as I puffed and wheezed and tried to grab a shoelace at a time. I fell farther and farther behind. The kids that lapped me laughed as they passed a pathetic kid, hopping up on alternating legs, trying to tuck in his shoelaces. My memory of the race stops there; I assume I just stopped walking and half-jogged the rest of the way. As for the high jump, I still had hope. I tried the backward Fosbury Flop, but I hit the bar on the lowest level and fell straight down onto the track, missing the landing mat completely. At least no friends or family that had come to see me.

We all got yellow "Jr. Olympics" T-shirts that many of my classmates wore proudly the next week at school. I buried mine in the back of my dresser. That week, a kid named Jamie Peters did an impression of my run and went hopping and skipping in front of the class as we lined up outside for the Pledge of Allegiance.[3] Ryan and Brendan were laughing at me as Jamie did his imitation of the chubby kid galloping, tripping, and grabbing at his shoes. My teacher—Buddhist Kramer—stood at the head of the line with his arms crossed. I looked at him with a plaintive look, pleading for the mocking to stop. He did nothing. The bell rang, and we all said the Pledge of Allegiance. Things kept sucking like this through fifth grade.

---

[3] A lot of guys were named Jamie in the late '80s. Where did they all go? I can't think of many senators or captains of industry today named Jamie.

X Marx the Spot

Some kids talk about the junior high or high school years being the worst of their lives. For me, it was my first years in elementary school. I remember wondering if I would ever make friends. At least by junior high, you probably already had the experience of making friends at some earlier point. You probably played at other people's houses and knew that you could probably find some clique that fit your social status. Not making friends from the very earliest school years marked the beginning of me spending years wondering why I wasn't like any of the other kids. I didn't have a meaningful relationship with anyone, and I didn't have the means to do so. I'd have to figure out how to fit in, and while some might find their answers on the knee of their granddad or in sage parental advice, I went to my own emotional standby: the formulaic family sitcom and power ballad.

I wanted to be like *Growing Pains'* Mike Seaver (a prezealot Kirk Cameron) or Mackenzie Astin (Sean's younger brother, who was the smart talking kid at Mrs. G's home for girls on *The Facts of Life*) or a young Zack Morris (Mark Paul Goselaar on an early incarnation of *Saved by the Bell* called *Good Morning, Miss Bliss* on the Disney Channel). At best, I was a more awkward Kevin Arnold from *The Wonder Years*, but without the dimples or voice over from Daniel Stern. As I became increasingly self-conscious, I spent more time in my room listening to the radio. I would sit on the floor, looking at *Where's Waldo?* books. I didn't like to read so the detailed picture books took my mind off of other things; plus, I needed to listen carefully to the lyrics of the adult contemporary soft rock that filled my afternoons. I would listen to anything by REO Speedwagon, Bad English, Damn Yankees, Don Henley (post-Eagles), and most of all—the crown jewel of '80s balladry—Richard Marx. I eventually came across enough money to buy Marx's *Repeat Offender* album and acquire my sister's old Walkman. I lay on my stomach, leafing through the *Where's Waldo?* books, deciphering the stories behind the songs like "Angelia," "Satisfied," "Children of the Night," and "Right Here Waiting." If I was in a particularly blue mood, I could listen to "Right Here Waiting" and start crying. I could also imagine myself rocking the elementary school talent show with the adult contemporary up-tempo "Satisfied." Or maybe I could sing

Marx's "Children of the Night," which was to runaway children what "Luka" was to abused women. I know my story has its own peculiarities, but I refuse to believe that there weren't other prepubescent boys that longed to be Richard Marx. Or at least dream of killing one of his songs at a talent show and leaving the girls swooning.

With the number of albums sold and videos played, albeit on VH1, which was, at the time, the adult-contemporary alternative to MTV, there have to be a number of men who received their formative lessons in pining for girls, their ideas about what was romantic and sincere and heartfelt, from the music of Richard Marx. After 1989's *Repeat Offender* (What was his offense, by the way? Breaking hearts? Pioneering hair styles? Mastering the synth bass?), he went downhill, but maybe we just grew up. Maybe his music—the song from *Anastasia* and the Christmas album that I cannot listen to— is striking a chord in the hearts of eight-year-old boys across the nation on their transistor radios, or Spotify, or YouTube. Perhaps there is an analog to vintage '80s Richard Marx today. I don't want to know about him, her, or them. I had my ideal of what was romantic and melancholy set then. And perhaps, between the ages of eight and eleven, Richard Marx and some of his musical compatriots made their mark on me. Sure, I would move onto the Smiths and Sunny Day Real Estate and the Pixies later. But for a few years, it was me, in my bedroom, reading the Sports Almanac and *Where's Waldo?* books. Had a bus hit Richard Marx when he was seventeen, I'm pretty sure I would have grown up with a very different picture of the things that I would obsess over for the next decade of my life.

I cannot overstate this. "Right Hear Waiting," "Angelia," "Satisfied," "Children of the Night," "Endless Summer Nights," "Hold on to the Nights"—these were the soundtrack to my life in my Walkman headphones getting ready for school, walking home from school, and spending weekends holed up in my bedroom.

Sure, you had Peter Cetera (post-Chicago, "Karate Kid II Theme" era). We had OMD and later (and a surprisingly much better solo) Don Henley. But I believe Richard Marx, despite the guffaws about his mullet and melodramatic videos, had to have had an effect on adolescent boys that we could never quantify with statistics.

But there are at least a few coincidences, which suggest I am not the only one who had their lives fundamentally changed by the words and melodies of Richard Marx.

For instance, in high school, I went to three dances at different schools that all had themes based on a song title by Richard Marx: "Endless Summer Nights," "Hold on to the Nights," and "Right Here Waiting." The last song and theme made the least sense, but it was certainly Marx's best ballad. I always thought that this was particularly strange. No one admitted to liking Richard Marx. But committees made up of cheerleaders and student body presidents and the like kept going back to the same well. Why is this strange or relevant? Because I believe that somewhere, at some point, Richard Marx—he of the quaffed wave and mullet hairstyle—was given some kind of strange gift not unlike those that were probably bestowed upon Paul McCartney, Mozart, and probably at least three of the original members of The Eagles. Unfortunately, Marx was unable to make anything timeless, except for a handful of us. I will still listen to *Repeat Offender* without a trace of irony. But it is stuck in 1988 and unless you happen to have had the experiences that some of us did in the late '80s, you will find his music somewhere on a scale between unlistenable and pathetic pabulum.

Richard Marx matters to us few, sort of how Neil Diamond means a lot to a handful of our parents. Go ahead and stop reading here and go to your favorite streaming music device and listen to the first weird synth chords of "Right Here Waiting" or the bad pseudo-rock guitar riff on "Satisfied" and then that drum machine and synth bass on "Endless Summer Nights."

Top 5 Richard Marx Songs

5. Children of the Night
4. Angelia
3. Hold on to the Nights
2. Endless Summer Nights
1. Right Here Waiting (You expected something else? This would be like picking a band other than the Beatles in a category of best bands out of Liverpool.)

I suppose all of this led to a number of things, one was a propensity for a kind of artificial longing for objects of affection that may or may not actually exist. Even if she was a man-eater, I would be right here waiting. It also lent itself to a lot of time alone and introspection. I thought that the ongoing dialogue with myself was peculiar to me. (Apparently, it's not; however, my slight mouthing of my internal dialogue with shifting eyebrows according to the inner discussion has been the subject of some mocking and curious stares.)

Bad Friend Gary

I would remain marinating in melancholy and alone most of the time, pining secretly after girls as I walked around the neighborhood and dreaming of soft rock stardom, but fate smiled upon me in the summer before sixth grade. I didn't have a growth spurt or suddenly learn to do "slicees" to become the king of the handball court. But a kid moved in a few houses down from me who had gone through a growth spurt and could do "slicees" and "waterfalls" and knew tricks from his hometown courts in Los Angeles like "open window" and "pac mans." And he swore to us that "bubblies" were perfectly legitimate. These were all bitchin' handball moves. Master them, and you could dominate a neighborhood socially. And Gary was famous for having changed the game of handball at Brywood Elementary School.

He was six feet tall, with a receding hairline. And in sixth grade. Rumor had it he was in a gang. He started this rumor. Sylvester, the other alpha dog at school, once challenged our new Odysseus to a fight. Most kids in my übersuburban and affluent home city of Irvine would never actually fight, but this new guy, during the second week, put Sylvester in a headlock and punched him in the face, breaking his nose and leaving us all with a purple and blue notice under Sylvester's eye. It read: a new top dog was in town.

CHAPTER 4
With a Little Help from My Friends

Or, Sixth-Grade Badass, Junior High Punching Bag, and Freshman Addict

A Soundtrack for Reading

1. With a Little Help from My Friends—The Beatles
2. Smells Like Teen Spirit—Nirvana
3. Raising Hell—Run-D.M.C.
4. White Lines—Grandmaster Flash and the Furious Five
5. Sheena Is a Punk Rocker—The Ramones
6. Tame—The Pixies
7. The Breaks—Kurtis Blow
8. Camels, Spilled Corona and the Sound of Mariachi Bands—J Church
9. Let Me Clear My Throat—DJ Kool
10. Jane Says—Jane's Addiction
11. Me Myself and I—De La Soul
12. So What'cha Want—Beastie Boys

We think boys are rude, insensitive animals but it is
not so in all cases. Each boy has one or two sensitive
spots, and if you can find out where they are located
you have only to touch them and you can scorch him
as with fire.

—Mark Twain

Gary has been called "Bad Friend Gary" since I first had to distinguish between him and all the other six-foot-tall sixth-grade ne'er-do-wells prone to misdemeanors named Gary from my hometown. He was Tony Soprano mixed with Farkus from *A Christmas Story*. Farkus is the bully that you probably only remember for his red hair and cackle. Gary is probably known primarily for the moniker he received from me and his eye rolls and smirks. But it does me well to remember that he wasn't just the antagonist in most of my stories from this time; he was also a real kid with real issues. He had moved from LA with his mom and left a group of friends to come to the monolithic planned city, recently named the safest in the country. When he got to Irvine, he was looking for a new posse. We didn't have "posses" here. No one lined up to greet him or join his club. So I became his posse, all of five feet, chubby, and filled with anxiety. I was like a mix between Little Stevie Van Zandt from *The Sopranos* (and the E Street Band) and the kid that followed Farkus around in *A Christmas Story*, who was mostly memorable for the height difference between he and Farkus and his coonskin hat. Now that Gary was the new alpha dog at school, walking around with him brought me instant credibility, at least in my eyes. More important, it meant that no bully could touch me. I gained a type of immunity that gave me a false sense of comfort around other kids. I had not actually become cooler, but I learned that if you act cool some people will start to believe it. I gained confidence and garnered some attention from my peers. Although I had to keep my soft-rock balladeer aspirations to myself, I could now talk about Run-D.M.C., Digital Underground, Aerosmith, and Mötley Crüe with the opinion makers by the handball courts. And with my strange ability to memorize quickly, I could hang with the biggest of fans and pretend I had always loved the Oakland hip hop scene, preferred Joe Perry's solo album, and tell the difference between Nikki Sixx and Mick Mars. I could still pursue my goal of becoming the

Mike-Seaver-meets-Zack-Morris character that television assured me would make me clever, popular with girls, and witty enough to get out of trouble with a quick excuse or a smile. I would, to my chagrin, remain much more of the Boner-meets-Screech in our recasting of my childhood for the late-1980s television movie version of my life.

In just one year, Gary would lead me to some of the most ridiculous, stupid, thoughtless, and criminal things I would ever do. He could easily be the villain of the first part of my life, but he was in the sixth grade. What the hell did he know? He is probably better remembered as a tragic figure. His mom ran an illegal childcare operation out of her place, so we had that in common.[1] His dad was nowhere to be found, and his mom's boyfriend was a guy named James. James was a bodybuilder whose claim to fame was his role in a prominent music video. He loved to remind us of this. Thinking about this, I was about as impressed with that then as I am now. He came from a broken home and never found footing before being thrust into a new town as the baby-faced man-child.

Once Gary decided, against my better inclinations, that we should go to the TMP. We abbreviated everything. If you said "Tustin Market Place" and were not talking to an adult, we knew you were a loser. Using its whole name was a shibboleth by which we could tell whether someone was a real insider. In North Irvine, this was an issue because of the . . . actually, I have no idea why this was a big deal. But in Orange County, where we didn't have any real problems, we feared outsiders. And earthquakes. And bees.

The original buildings that made up the shopping center still exist, and to this day, I still refer to it as the TMP, which makes me laugh to myself a little each time. My parents had two inviolable rules: there was to be no *Felix the Cat* on television and no going to the TMP. Really? Two rules. But being that there were only two, I guess I figured they must be important. My mom thought that the black-and-white cat and his bag of tricks had a bad attitude, and she would not tolerate him in our house. We obeyed. Never mind that my friend Jesse, in the second grade, would bring a video to my house about a nurse who was apparently too warm to keep her clothes on around her patient. We watched that curious medical relationship unfold on

---

[1] My mom ran an unlicensed daycare in our home, FYI.

screen with turned stomachs and a guilty curiosity. I apparently had no prohibition nor warning against smut. But the animated cat with a bad attitude? Never. They could have used what few rules they had more judiciously. Once my dad made my sister turn off an episode of *Beverly Hills, 90210* because Brenda and Dylan were going to have sex. I didn't care much for the show, but the prohibition against it led to it becoming my favorite show. Seriously, ask me anything about any of the ten seasons. I cannot be stumped. This and *Saved by the Bell* are more responsible for shaping my view of school, my teen years, and my views of parents and principles and grown-up life than these two shows. When I took my first job back in the United States at the place where the high school scenes in 90210 were filmed, I wish I hadn't been so drunk as to rarely show up and not take any pictures recreating scenes from the show. I could have been, and maybe should have been, drunk to do the latter.

We weren't allowed to walk or ride bikes to the TMP; I have no idea why not. Or why I took this rule as somehow inviolable. The not riding bikes part was an unnecessary stipulation, since I only had one bike growing up, and that one had since been stolen. I was thus relegated to walking—I was afraid of skateboards—or riding on pegs on the back wheels of friend's bikes. I held onto the rule, most likely because I was afraid of having to ride a skateboard or on pegs. I told Gary and a few friends that I couldn't be seen walking down the mile-long stretch of road that led to the shopping center. Gary suggested we walk through the giant run-off sewage pipes that ran between the empty city block connecting us to marketplace. A couple minutes into the darkness of the tunnel, I shouted, "Homeless guy!"

We all ran as fast as we could out of the pipe, across the embankment and onto the sidewalk. Huffing and puffing with our hands on our knees, we started speculating about the nature of the homeless guy. Living where we did, "homeless guy" was to us what "active shooter" is to people in big cities. I can't remember why I yelled, "Homeless guy!" I probably saw a cardboard box or a shopping cart. I may have just made it up because I was too scared to go farther into the dark tunnel. If you ever start to feel like my story is too tragic, please remember that we were so white and middle class that the prospect of a homeless person being in our vicinity immediately stopped us in our tracks. It could always be worse, dear reader.

Gary decided that to avoid possible homeless people interactions, we would ride bikes, instead. I thought we were going to go to the record store. It was a Tower Records, and it was the only thing you would go to the TMP for unless you wanted Taco Bell or Toys "R" Us, which were both overlit, smelled curious, and were generally janky enough that they were relegated to these shopping centers just past the darkness on the edge of the town. Tower Records would be the main reason I would break the "No TMP" rule every weekend. I would spend entire days in there, looking through CDs and making mental notes of who was on what label and which albums various bands recorded. Curiously, as we got to the TMP, we headed to the Toys "R" Us. I couldn't understand what we would do there. More curiously, Gary rode over to the exit, rather than the entrance. He told me:

"When I hand you the box, just get on my bike and start riding home fast."

"But how will you get home?"

"Don't worry about it," he replied.

"Don't worry about it" was said in a dismissive, condescending tone. It was a common phrase he would use whenever my conscience would make a strange appearance and question what we were doing.

Gary waited until someone exited, and then he straddled the automatic sliding door and grabbed boxes of Upper Deck baseball cards, handed me one, and told me to ride fast. I looked behind me and saw that Gary had taken a bike that was sitting out in front of the store. We ended up with three boxes of Upper Deck's 1989 inaugural season of baseball cards. These were easily 150 bucks apiece. We rifled through the packs and found two Ken Griffey Jr. rookie cards as well as the "Rising Star" cards of Brien Taylor and Ben McDonald. (If you recognize either name, you know why it is funny we kept them locked in thick plastic card carriers.) Gary had just stolen over $500 worth of baseball cards. And a bike. I was horrified and impressed. I took a few of my ill-gotten cards and traded them for the Topps 86 Wally Joyner rookie card and a few other Angels, like Nolan Ryan—a "Legends" hologram card—and a Dean Chance card from the '60s.

I can understand the brash confidence of a sixth-grade kid that would commit such a crime. But the parts that still make me wonder are those things we did that had no real payoff. These were those things that didn't take much effort, and gave little payout, except maybe a chuckle or something to scratch an itch. For example, no one lived in the house next to Gary, so we would routinely climb the fence and content ourselves by peeing on the grass in the backyard. But when we were especially mischievous, we learned that the house next door could be entered if we jimmied a screwdriver into a corner of a window panel and pushed out the glass. We had an entire home to ourselves; we could have made that the ultimate fort. We could have hid the omnipresent gentlemen's magazines and our stolen goods in the cupboards. We had, for about six months, a vacant house all to ourselves, yet we decided it would be best to use as our own personal walk-in urinal. We thought it was hilarious to pee on the carpets. I can't count how many stories from my youth involve peeing on things for effect. To intimidate a kid we didn't like, we peed on his front lawn with him watching us and shouting. We could have used the backyard for most any purpose as well. Even as a pissing spot, it would have been better than what we did. We would take our stolen goods to the backyard to inspect or sit back there if we wanted to try smoking or drinking. But we smoked and drank to little success. This marks the only time in my life that I didn't impress my friends with my uncanny ability to smoke and drink anyone under the table. I couldn't finish my first tumbler of vodka and pretended to drink what I tossed into the bushes. Cigarettes seemed like a dumb way to waste lighter fluid. I was twelve. I was more interested in setting things on fire.

We tried the "magnifying glass + sun + spider" equation to no avail. But we heard that there was a better solution: Aquanet, a ubiquitous aerosol hair spray from the '80s. By sparking a flame and spraying Aquanet in the target's direction, we could make our own blowtorch. We had heard that the flame could "travel back into the can and blow up," but we did it a few times, and it never happened. So we were cool; no caution would be necessary. We tried using two cans of aerosol, two lighters, and we figured we had exhausted all possible options. Until we learned about WD-40. WD-40 worked just as well as Aquanet, and so we found friends who had dads with garages and rustled up a few cans. Once we saw how the liquid worked, we decided to douse the grass in the liquid and then light it. It worked. Very well. We stomped on it and poured our sodas on it until it was small enough that we could run next door and were able to fetch cups of water to put it out completely. But the smell got to Gary's mom, who came yelling and told Gary to go straight to his room. Gary's mom turned to me: "I know your mom is strict, so I won't tell her. But you are grounded with Gary for the next two weekends."

I remember thinking, *I have to come over here for the next two weekends and sit in Gary's bedroom and watch TV and play video games?*

There would be no plea bargain; I took the punishment and . . . well, spent the next two weekends like I spent most weekends. Except this time, I had a surrogate mom around who was engaged enough to pencil out a traditional grounding. And who told her my mom was strict? Was it the Felix-the-Cat thing?

If there were to be no real consequences, we figured that we could make mischief for mischief's sake. The empty house next door had a garage with a plastic door but a main front panel made of composite wood. We knew that by rubbing steel wool against the wood, we could make a mark. Or more.

I don't know who instigated it, but I had started to scratch out a giant *F* on the door. It worked brilliantly. I etched out a large *U* next to it and beamed with self-assuredness and pride. I had just started to crest the top of the *C* when a neighbor ran over yelling. He was a cop. He told us that he knew we were "behind things" and that I had better scratch out my two and a half letters. I specifically remember the police officer using the ominous language of us being "behind things." Like what? The death of Paulie Scrimatone from Philly or an illicit black market of goods in North Irvine? I was more confused than afraid. But my next encounter with a policeman would be the time I would certainly come to respect the long arm of Johnny law, and it began the demise of a brief relationship with Gary that was filled with bad decisions, insecurity, and questionable parenting. It would also end the brief and comically nefarious duo that must have been a sight to behold: one dude a slight, six-foot-tall twelve-year-old, with the face of a small child and the receding hairline of a forty-year-old, and a baby-faced, flush-cheeked, barely five-foot-tall twelve-year-old, wearing baggy clothes with a head so full of hair gel that it shone like an onyx. My hair was always just a bit too long, and I hated having curls, so I used extrastrength gel and Aquanet to make it sit still.

It was the spring of 1990, and I had been invited to my first boy/girl birthday party. It was at Carissa Stone's house. She was popular, albeit popular by association. She was friends with Summer Redstone. Carissa was like Summer's newly pubescent bouncer, keeping the wrong crowd away from Summer at recess and lunch. The issue of girls and puberty was deeply contested for the boys on the Brywood Elementary playground. Once, on an episode of *Roseanne*, a subplot involved Sara Gilbert's character and her period. This led to an intense debate as to what "the period" was. Someone suggested it involved bleeding. We laughed that one off. Gross. Never. Also, we didn't have sex education until seventh grade. But the lure of girls and their mysterious ways was one of my driving motivators.

Being invited to this party meant that I had made it. I would be at the same place as all the Mikes, and Jakes, and Brads. And of course, Summer Redstone. Her name always had to be uttered with both forename and surname. It was like the opposite of Cher. You had to say the whole thing, like it was a spell that invoked the gods of prepubescent Eros. It was always the quick answer to questions that began, "Who would . . . ?" or "If you could only . . . ?" She would always be one of the four marriage options in the game of MASH. Not until Samantha Segerstrom did a name require not only both names but also for it to be said in hushed tones swirling alongside some kind of rumor, and pubescent nerves, and ill-timed, coincidental erections. A quick note to any women reading this book: the ill-timed erection was the ultimate fear of all junior high boys. It mostly involved neurons misfiring, our bodies lurching and kicking into adulthood. But if you were sitting in homeroom and got an erection, you had to keep your head down so as to not be called on to stand or go to the front of the class. You had to pray there was enough time in class for you to sit awkwardly and wait for it to go away. Salvation by the bell in such cases became social damnation if you were unlucky. The only analogy I can think of is realizing there is a police car behind you after you've had a few too many or expired tags or an unregistered firearm. In such situations, your pupils dilate and you sit up straight, wipe a bead of sweat off your forehead, and hope that it all passes without incident.

I didn't have the right clothes to go to my first mixed-gender, hormonally charged birthday party, and no one matched my awkward body shape from whom I might borrow clothes. I was too thin for the fat kids' and too fat for the thin kids'. I begged my mom to take me to the Millers Outpost at the TMP, where I promised I would be quick and find something on sale. I bought the clothes, and wasn't sure if they would fit if they were washed, so I insisted on wearing them straight out of the bag, creases and all. It was a magenta t-shirt with a pocket and high collar (it was a shirt that had a faux turtleneck that looked less turtle and more "casual priest"). My shorts exposed a little too much of my embarrassing thighs and white legs. I went shopping for just the right clothes and ended up buying something that I would probably never wear again and probably looked more foolish on me than anything I already had in my closet.

As the day grew closer, I was also tormented by the fear that Carissa would open each gift and announce, to a crowd of Jakes, Jamies, and Brads, who bought what. I had little money on me but knew I had to get something that would stick out in her mind or, more precisely, Summer's mind. I had no interest in Carissa and no shot at Summer, but if Summer approved of me, I figured it would open the gate for the C-list sixth-grade girls to try to date me for strategic social reasons. I had to pick my gift wisely.

The Wherehouse (a cleverly titled, now defunct record store) had a wall of cassette singles from the current week's Rick Dees Weekly Top 40. I knew what was generally popular, but my secret jams were all from the contemporary soft-rock category. I figured I would get something cool there, as I didn't think "The End of the Innocence" by Don Henley would pass (although, it is still one hell of a song). I remember looking at the covers on Extreme's "More than Words" and Tesla's "Signs." I had to think of this not as an aesthetic choice but one of purely Machiavellian designs. If I went too soft, I could end up looking like a wuss. If I went too obscure, I would be forgotten. I couldn't afford anything but a single, so I needed to choose carefully. Hitting something in the narrow window between Roxette and the Pixies seemed difficult, as I tend to go to the extreme on both sides of most continuums. For example, I never drank socially nor did I smoke much weed. I chugged cheap vodka and did cocaine. Middle ground is for the weak. Ask Don Henley.

I ended up getting her Gerardo's "Rico Suave," a song half-sung, half-rapped by a Latino playboy, with his shirt off and long locks of curly black hair running down his brown oily torso. It was such a hit, Carissa unwrapped it and put it on during the party. Everything was coming up roses. My full ascent from carpet wetter, to Junior Olympic flame out, to weird sidekick, to now actual popularity was close at hand. And then Gary decided we should steal everyone's candy and leave early.

We started by quickly grabbing everyone's party bags and dumping their contents into our own. Gary went inside to use the bathroom, I presumed, and came out with a handful of brightly colored after-dinner mints. He told me there was candy inside the house, in the living room and on the shelves. As we raided these primarily aesthetic grown-up party glass bowls, Carissa's dad, a policeman as he reminded us often, found us out and started to ask what we thought we were doing. Gary gave him his "eff you old man" stare, and we soon found ourselves on the street, walking home empty-handed. I was unable to bask in the glory of my brilliantly chosen gift of the cassette single by a "Spanglish" rapper without a shirt. I had grasped the gold ring only to have it snatched away from me. I walked home with Gary, but he didn't seem to share my melancholy mood. He thought it was funny. I had just found myself exiled from the Promised Land I had only just entered. This was a terrible day.

But it got worse.

On the way home, we walked down a street in our housing development with tall wooden fences separating backyards from the street. As we walked by them, Gary bet me that he could kick in one of the fences. I decided to take the bait and bet him. He gave himself a running start and then kicked through at least three 2 × 4's exposing a major hole into a backyard with both a dog and man barbecuing. We both started running, and obviously, due to his size, Gary led the way. We ran around a corner toward a cul-de-sac before Gary yelled at me to turn back. By this time, the man had headed us off in his car. Gary claimed that our friend Justin kicked in the fence and had run the other way. Gary used his full name, Justin Braddock. This was both a dick move and also set the precedent for me thinking we had to use both first and last name of a real person. The man asked for our names and Gary gave him the name, first and last, of another classmate, Mike Santiago. I remember thinking that this could lead to problems from them and then us. When he asked me my name, I could only think of the small group of boys that hung around with Justin and Mike Santiago. I panicked and picked the name of one of the boys in that group. I told the man my name was Peter Chang.

Not only was this one of the Asian kids in our class, it was the name of the toughest Asian kid at our school. Were there a suburban, sixth-grade syndicate of the Yakuza, he would have been it. I immediately realized what I had done, so I offered the man more information in the hope of throwing him off our trail. I told him we went to Venado Middle School. But, not only did I not look anywhere near ready for Middle School, Venado was a school for kids in a different part of town. I went to sleep with a knot in my stomach. The following Monday, the ominous feedback rang out from the room speaker that let us know some school-wide announcement was coming. I sat through a few of these as we were called to salute the flag, reminded to bring cans to school, and told that student government election packets were ready to pick up. And as I had let my guard down once the afternoon came, a postlunch announcement rang out; we were called by name and told to come to the office. Had I not since gotten over my fear of school toilets, I would have surely soiled myself. We walked up to Mr. Cunningham's office and into the conference room where two policemen were waiting. Anyone who described the two of us would have easily been told where we went to school, and I suspect Carissa's dad being a cop led to this strange shakedown of two sixth graders. We were asked if we kicked in the fence. Gary defiantly said no. I shook my head and mouthed no. Gary was sent back to the waiting area as I stayed in the room. I noticed the handcuffs on the police. I figured I would end up in juvenile hall. They didn't say anything to me, and I started to breathe heavily and dart my eyes nervously across the room. It seemed like five minutes, but was probably about thirty seconds. I couldn't hang with the impressive shake down and interrogation from the IPD.

"It was Gary. (*Sobbing.*) Gary kicked the fence not me IswearhediditandthenheliedbutIthoughtitwasabadideabutstillhetold me. . . ." I ran words together and tripped over my tongue. I was sweaty and shaking and terrified of juvenile hall. I snapped like a dry twig. I couldn't stand the heat. I was excused and let go back to my class. Gary got in trouble but either didn't know I ratted on him or didn't care based on the reaction I got from him later that day. I didn't see him for a few weeks, but when I did, he was with Jason Parks, another diminutive ne'er-do-well with pale skin and oily hair. I never realized the parallels between me and Jason. I don't know if I was jealous or relieved. I was probably a little bit of both.

On the Cusp of Seventh Grade (and Communal Showers)

It was the end of sixth grade, and my rise to the orbit of the kids who went snow skiing together and wore new clothes to match their new shoes and bikes and rollerblades was now out of reach. I was so close. Carissa's birthday party could have been the catapult into popularity I thought it was when she had opened the Rico Suave cassette single. But now I was without a troubled six-foot-tall organism for my would-be parasitical self. Gary ditched me for a similarly prepubescent henchman. It was like being the original mom on *The Fresh Prince of Bel-Air* or the original older sister on *Roseanne*. When people used to be written off a show, they simply made it part of the plot. Valerie Harper, of the self-titled and eponymously named television show she created, *Valerie*, was written off of her own show as the victim of a helicopter crash. (It was only later that someone told me they didn't actually kill her in a helicopter crash; I was honestly concerned and angry about NBC judging us for content and questionable morals.) I had hit the chute and dropped down to a level of eating my lunch in the classroom. I was an outcast. And this was on the eve of the summer before junior high. A summer filled with the dread of having no friends, rumors of public showers, and new mythic names of boys from other schools who had done everything from break the junior high's Coke machine open and stealing the money to allegedly almost burning down the school with Molotov cocktails.

With my small group of friends now having banished me to solitude, I spent that summer working as a volunteer at the after-school day care center I had attended in elementary school. (I can't let this pass; I went to an after-school day care, even though my mom ran her own.) This was the summer I would start to find random kids to hang out and try to impress them with the amount of music trivia or sports statistics I knew or how I was willing to go out with their friends to make them like me and get a boost of confidence from a girl that I might talk with a few times before ignoring them until they went away.

I spent that summer from May to early fall watching my Angels fall out of contention by the All Star break, shooting baskets at a local park with an underinflated ball; just one of those little needles used to inflate balls would have been the gift of my childhood. My football, soccer ball, and basketball were always just slightly deflated, enough that it took the joy out of playing with them. That, and I rarely had someone to play with. Also, the pump that we did have was only good for things with inner tubes like . . . bicycles. Of which, I had my one and only years earlier. I started walking around the neighborhood, and as we moved every year but stayed in the same area—for which I have a suspicion why—this was a new neighborhood. I was close to a Sam Goody and a bookstore and a SavOn. I could rifle through cassette tapes and sports and music magazines and at least learn about what books existed, even if I wouldn't read a full book until my freshman year of high school. As the MTV Video Music Awards approached, I remembered being really excited at the prospect of Arsenio Hall hosting, live performances by Guns 'N Roses and Paula Abdul, and maybe a Michael Jackson sighting. But I knew that the VMAs were the day before the first day of seventh grade. Every commercial teaser for the show, with new bands being added, was another jab in the side reminding me that junior high was coming.

Thankfully, it didn't start out all bad. Gary and his new cronies would mock me in homeroom, and I was beat up by Reggie Smith for allegedly ripping his sweatshirt, but it turned out you didn't have to shower after PE. That alone made up for everything else. I walked laps around the junior high for the first few weeks of seventh grade with my head down waiting for the bell to send us back to class. Eventually, I met a few kids in my PE class that I had impressed with my football skills. Rather, my pretending to walk off the field every so often, but behind the line of scrimmage, and then bolting up the field uncovered for a deep pass and an easy touchdown.

After a while, I started to hang out with this group of kids who were decidedly not into Richard Marx, but rather the Ramones, Pixies, pre–*Joshua Tree* U2, and mix tapes made by older brothers that would be copied and spread around, with bands like Christie Front Drive, J Church, and Jawbreaker. Any anxiety I had trying to make new friends went away with a combination of these facts: these boys weren't exactly upper-tier popular, they liked sports and I could recall game box scores and stats better than anyone, and my jumping headfirst into this postpunk college rock world and spending time trying to find any information on them that I could at record stores and in the *Rolling Stone* and *Spin* magazines in the library made me the encyclopedia and arbiter of all music- and sports-related debates. All this and, of course, booze and whatever substance we could find to get high.

The early years of my substance abuse will be recounted later; but, I stopped using almost *anything* that *anyone* I respected stood against—even going so far as to claiming to be "straight edge," and becoming a vegetarian—thanks to a mix of Ian Mackaye of Minor Threat and the Smiths' *Meat Is Murder* album. This brief fit of sobriety sprang from my strange relationship with the church (also a chapter for later) and a few new friends at a church who I thought would disapprove of my substance abuse. It was unfair for me to suggest that these church kids thought of themselves as better than me, as many of them did not. But I still felt the need to keep the relationship with my old friends, just in case. With connections back at the school across town, most of whom are still around years after my depression and addiction led me away from them to the brink of suicide and back to something resembling normal.

"Here Kitty, Kitty"

What led me to jump from the group of guys that appreciated my sports knowledge and musical aesthetic to a new friendless existence involved hallucinogens, a cat, and a sexually explicit rumor.

The guys that I got drunk and high with decided one night that I had absconded with a cat into the bathroom. Actually, I freaked out and ran into the bathroom, away from the cat, while on a bad trip. This quickly morphed into a story told among peers about my having intimate relations with the cat. Seriously, this is what these ninth graders came up with. It led to stories of me finding local cats, injecting them with a sedating serum, and then having my way with them. The guys would make cat sounds and press their thumb through their first two fingers, mimicking the injecting of a needle, and fall over each other laughing until they got distracted or bored and then walk away. A number of other kids only saw that this made me turn red and angry and on the brink of tears, and so they started to do it too. By the end of ninth grade, I couldn't walk around school without hearing cat sounds and seeing the thumb and forefinger motion. For the first time in my life, I truly believed that the only options I had were to end my own life or end one of theirs. I remember kneeling down to get books from my locker and burning so hot with shame and rage. If I close my eyes, even now, I can vividly remember the exact moment I was convinced that someone would have to die. And I wasn't the type with the means or guts to do anything to anyone else. But I was also too afraid to kill myself in any violent manner.

I remember hearing that if you touched lead, it could kill you. And while I didn't work out the illogic of my train of thought, I decided one day that I would walk through the gym right after the lunch bell and rub my hands all over the weights—I assumed they were lead—and promptly lick my hands. Afterward, I went to sixth-period biology waiting for something to happen. I figured that the lead would have to make it into my blood stream. This might take a day or two. I remember walking around aimlessly that afternoon. And the next day, I ditched school, so that when I did keel over, I would be alone. I listened to my mix tapes of ballads about longing for girls and any other form of affection that I knew I could never experience. I still had Richard Marx, but my tapes now included brooding stuff too, like the Smiths, the Cure and other sad-sack post-punk British pop. I would periodically sit down when my stomach started to hurt (obviously nerves) until the weekend came, and I was convinced that I must have done it wrong. And then I realized that if touching weights could kill you, weightlifting would either be a foolish sport banned by Western nations or else my science was bad.

Nonetheless, my suicide attempt, as lame as it was, gave me a new approach to life. I knew I had the choice to die, and I didn't. Within the next few weeks, I started joining in on a conversation with two girls that I often overheard talking about music and movies.

Here Comes Your Man

Jessica and Kim knew about Christie Front Drive, early Green Day, and a number of local bands I hadn't heard of. Once, when they mentioned J Church, I told them how the band got its name after a BART stop in San Francisco. I probably claimed that their song "Jamie" was the reason I was a vegetarian (or at least planned to be one at the time). They were impressed enough to let me come with them to Dairy Queen in Kim's car after school. The three of us spent our sophomore year with a curious affection triangle. This was not quite a love triangle, but some strange hormonal vibes were resonating among the three of us. I would walk to their jobs, and we would go thrift store shopping and go to all age shows where bands like No Doubt and Sublime were just starting to hit big, inspiring hundreds of other bands to flood all ages clubs all throughout Orange County.

Meanwhile, on nights that I wasn't hanging out with them, I would find myself out anywhere I could find people. I wanted a clean, well-lit place. I wanted to go somewhere with people and light. I was maturing beyond the saccharin longing for "Endless Summer Nights" and now vacillating between the morose idea of dying in a double decker bus crash with the Smiths and the detached irony of Orange County third-wave ska bands, singing about not being cool.

When I met Anne, who loved the Smiths, and Brent, whose friends frequented the all-age clubs to hear new bands, I decided that I would latch onto them, and they, graciously, didn't mind being older than me. They went to a local church youth group that I would occasionally hang around, since my sister went. They all went to the high school across town. So that summer, I decided I would transfer to their school. Brent drove me to the school office—I wouldn't get my license until a few weeks before school started—and I asked for the paperwork needed to transfer. I was briefly interrogated but somehow answered their questions satisfactorily, so they handed me the paperwork I needed to give my parents. I forged signatures, then turned the paperwork in. Then just days before the first day of school, I told my incredulous mother that I was attending the school across town.

And just like that, amid the parallel stories of acting, drinking, and serial dating, I was on my way to the intersection of popularity, girls, the church, and a stint of sobriety. But all the fear and anxiety and lack of intimacy and early-onset depression and didn't magically go away. In fact, it never has completely vanished, but at least I was on the road to finding real intimacy and real peace. It only took a few dozen false starts and foolish paths to get there.

CHAPTER 5
Jesus, Etc.

Or, Finding Hope amid Games of Red Rover, Lock-ins, and Summer Camp

A Soundtrack for Reading

1. Jesus, Etc.—Wilco

2. Jesus Walks—Kanye West

3. Jesus Wants Me for a Sunbeam—the Vaselines (or "Jesus Doesn't Want Me for a Sunbeam," a cover by Nirvana)

4. Personal Jesus—Johnny Cash (covering Depeche Mode)

5. Jesus' Blood Never Failed Me Yet—Tom Waits

6. Jesus Is Just Alright—The Doobie Brothers

7. Jesus Christ Was an Only Child—Modest Mouse

8. Jesus Saves, I Spend—St. Vincent

9. Jesus Wrote a Blank Check—Cake

10. Jesus, I/Mary, Star of the Sea—Zwan

11. Jesus—Velvet Underground

12. Jesus Fever—Kurt Vile

> *I didn't go to religion to make me happy. I always knew*
> *a bottle of Port would do that. If you want a religion*
> *to make you feel really comfortable, I certainly don't*
> *recommend Christianity.*
>
> —C. S. Lewis

The scariest thing to reveal is that which renders you completely bare. Alcoholism, suicide, searching for something lost through substances and girlfriends, and living a double life are all difficult to come to terms with, but I no longer identify myself with these things. I am not above them, and I certainly don't think I'm immune from them. The monsters and demons of madness and despair are ever-present. They are my monsters, yes. But they are not *me*. On a cosmic level, I have come to believe that everything is going to be OK.

But what gives me the confidence to write something that bold? Something that contrary to human experience? It is the thing that gives me the most confidence and also the most fear. Religion, specifically the sort of Christianity that seeks freedom in the grace, peace, and hope of a world reconciled to God through the way of Jesus.

I had worked through a number of drafts for this book with very little reference to religion. I wrote about my experience with church and my baptism, but I shied away from writing specifically what I believe.

I had various reasons for doing this. First, I thought that it might put some people off. I thought that it might pigeonhole this work as some kind of apologetic or work of Christian subculture. I write this with all due respect to the father of memoirs, Augustine of Hippo, whose *Confessions* (AD 397–400) is the first modern autobiographical story about struggling with the self and the restlessness of a human heart that has yet to rest in the peace of God.

Second, I figured that if this became a "religious" book, it would have to withstand the scrutiny of the church. And thus, like any group of people with a social norm, it might bring criticism. This isn't an "I once was lost, but now am found" type of "testimony." So why invite scrutiny?

Third, and closest to the heart of the matter, I feared writing about any specifically religious tenets because it is scary to admit you believe something that appears ridiculous. To write as if I had anything to say about transcendent truth is off-putting not just to others but also to me. But Beth Anne and Jeff convinced me that if I wanted to give an honest account of my life, my religious convictions—which allow me to actually believe that everything is going to be OK—have to play a role in this story about monsters and hope and failure.

I have my bachelor's degree in theology. Some people don't know this because I took later degrees in history and politics. Sometimes I forget about my undergraduate degree myself. That was a long time ago. And I messed with my brain a good deal in subsequent years. When I get into something, I get into it. I didn't get into theology like a zealot ringing doorbells. Rather, I tried to learn the subject matter as quickly and thoroughly as possible.[1] Classically, faith involves (1) knowledge, (2) assent, and (3) trust. Intellectually, I hit the books hard. As an undergraduate, I got the knowledge part down. As I studied Christianity, I came to believe it. That is, I assented to its claims. The third step in this is to actually trust that it is true and true for you, specifically. Let's slow down and stay with the first two. Comprehension of the basic points was easy enough. Got it. Belief? Yeah, that wasn't too hard. Evidence for a historical Jesus and a reading of the Bible that emphasizes the radical grace of God, demonstrated through the bloody execution of God's son, to redeem the world? That sounded kind of cool.

I'm not ashamed of confessing what I believe. I do not, however, hold to a hollow, generic, or creedless faith. I recite the Apostles' Creed. I had my sons baptized.

I believe in the communion of Saints
The forgiveness of sins
The resurrection of the body
And the life Everlasting, Amen.

The Christian message—which I believe to be truth with a capital *T*, despite its having been hijacked by social commentators and moral crusaders—is the thing that gives me hope through suffering.

---

[1] I did take a class at a college where we were supposed to actually go door to door in twos or threes. This was *required*. My group would always include two guys (now pastors!) who would leave with me, and we would go to Outback Steakhouse and get a bloomin' onion and a few beers. I do not feel guilty about this.

My faith is not a comfort blanket. I have doubts and find it hard to pray. Jesus does not always seem to be nice in the Gospels; he demands too much and rebukes too often. When he's not speaking about astounding grace, Saint Paul sometimes seems to be the kind of moral crusader I loathe in modern society. Parts of the Old Testament seem weird.

There is a part of me that believes, *because* it sounds absurd, *because* it is contrary to my nature to hope. If my belief system fit too nicely with the way I saw the world, I would probably ditch it. For I would soon realize that I had made it up. This good news, the Gospel, the radically upside-down logic of Jesus is contrary to most things I experience. Consider my favorite parable:

The Parable of the Pharisee and the Tax Collector (Revised Standard Version)

He also told this parable to some who trusted in themselves that they were righteous and despised others: "Two men went up into the temple to pray, one a Pharisee and the other a tax collector. The Pharisee stood and prayed thus with himself, 'God, I thank thee that I am not like other men, extortioners, unjust, adulterers, or even like this tax collector. I fast twice a week, I give tithes of all that I get.' But the tax collector, standing far off, would not even lift up his eyes to heaven, but beat his breast, saying, 'God, be merciful to me a sinner!' I tell you, this man went down to his house justified rather than the other; for every one who exalts himself will be humbled, but he who humbles himself will be exalted."

A while back, I was going to get a tattoo of an old black-and-white woodcut of the tax collector with his head bowed. But the idea behind that tattoo would be radical mercy in the light of suffering: *misericordia* or pity, in a noncondescending way. Eventually, I took another route. I found my favorite rendering of a crucifix and had it tattooed on my forearm. The crucifix is not one that I picked out of a book at random or liked for purely aesthetic reasons. It is the centerpiece from Matthias Grunewald's Isenheim Altarpiece. It was originally painted for the children's ward of a hospital, during an outbreak of the plague in the fifteenth century. It is among the first to depict a *suffering* God. When my tattoo artist, Eric Jones, was working on it, he said, "Man, his face is fucked up . . . not the way I drew it, but the way it is." Yeah, that's the point.

Christ's arms are elongated and torqued as they writhe on the cross, his head bloodied and bowed. An emaciated, limp body hangs from two nailed hands. Ironically, though I'm often reluctant to talk about Christianity, I put this on the most prominent place on my left arm. Sometimes it gets stares or awkward looks. At other times, it leads to heavy conversations about life, death, and faith. None of my tattoos is *meant* to be a conversation starter. They are aesthetic pieces that have special significance for me.

An acquaintance once asked about my forearm crucifix. I told her it was an old piece of art and that I could identify with the idea of suffering. I didn't launch into an apologetic or attempt to prove the veracity of the Gospels. It was simply a way to identify myself as a fellow traveler, struggling along with life, on my way to the grave.

That I came to belief at all has been one of the more surprising things about my life. The idea of church was never odious to me. I was a white, middle-class suburban kid. Weren't we all Christians? Didn't the bearded guy from the painting decree that the modern white middle-class American were the new chosen people? The WASP was the new Jew. This was the '80s. Reagan and the moral majority were on top. My family made cameos in churches occasionally. We were sort of like Jewish families who throw up a menorah and stay home from work on Yom Kippur but eat shellfish without thinking twice. My parents liked church so long as it didn't require too much mental energy. They considered themselves part of the American evangelicalism that pervaded the late twentieth century, but they weren't going to wait in line for anything. They were into church like I am into the Coen brothers' movies. I'll watch *Blood Simple* or *Fargo* and start extolling their greatness with an evangelical zeal. But then I remember that I am implicitly approving of *Intolerable Cruelty* and *The Ladykillers*. So I cool off on them until I watch *The Big Lebowski* again, and it is back to the church of Joel and Ethan. But I'm not waiting in line for the premiere only to get duped by *Burn after Reading*. Jesus and the Coen brothers can be great. I just don't want them to get too pushy, preachy, or demanding of my time. Plenty of shiny-toothed youth pastors stopped by schools at lunch, basketball courts, and rec centers to invite us to their church, which tended to use mountain or water imagery and sometimes a verb associated with fire. Here are a few examples: The Rock, The River, Ignite. Those names don't make me want to come see what it's all about. "A rock? What an interesting metaphor. What kind of 'river' is this? Is it dangerous? Shallow? And Ignite . . . hmmm . . . were slacks a bad idea? Do I need to wear nonflammable clothes, just in case?" I tend to prefer doing nothing instead of something, so I tended to never go to these churches. Unless girls were involved.

In the second grade, a local youth group was looking for kids who were interested in being part of a stage production. I wasn't interested, but a girl I liked was. Her name was Jessie, a fourth grader and one of the most popular girls at school. I know this because, when *Good Morning, Miss Bliss* started, Zack's best friend was a girl named Jessie (and yes, this would become *Saved by the Bell*). So Jessie and her friends were auditioning for the stage production: a church musical. Seriously. There was a church musical. Who knew there was such a thing? I auditioned and got one of the lead parts. But since my stature was low and my vocal range was high, I was to play the role of the baby gorilla. The baby gorilla was part of a family of gorillas that were given the task of teaching a young girl how they would never want to evolve into humans, and thus anyone or anything that taught against a young earth and literal six-day creationism was off the table. Today I have a variety of problems with this production's approach to science, evangelism, and dramatic art. But back then, the biggest problem I had with it was that I had to wear a cumbersome and hot gorilla costume, complete with a diaper and pacifier. Jessie played my mother. I was in a diaper. Damn.

But I got to spend time with fourth graders, of whom Jessie and her friend were the ringleaders. I hung around. And as a pudgy, short baby gorilla, with the voice of a eunuch, I endeared myself to them. I still remember memorizing my lines and the lyrics to the songs. I can't remember my son's birthdays, or how old I am, or when to leave the office. But the first stanza I sang as a solo? Easy.

For people, family life is the pits.
Gorilla kids are grown up, by the time they're six.
Theirs hang around until they are teenaaaage.
They're the crazy animals who should be in a caaage.

I've got more.

Why would a fella, whose got it made,
swinging from the treetops, living in the shade
munchin' food that's fresh and free, breathing jungle air
trade his handsome [something] for one whose lost his hair?

It is called the *Creation Sensation* if you want to look for it. It is terrible. I think there was a VHS cassette of it somewhere, if it wasn't lost in the fire.[2] But it kept me hanging around the church, because I got adulation—if not from Jessie, from other kids who otherwise would want nothing to do with an awkward chubby kid that had just started going to school.

I went to a Catholic church after that because they let me play, at no charge, on the Little League team they sponsored. After the season, I had my own personal reformation and abandoned the Catholics for the Protestants, who had a summer camp and would let me go for free if I joined their camp. (Please note this is tongue-in-cheek as I had no clue, nor did I care about which team was which.)

Hearing I was going to church, my neighbors took me to a Protestant church of the charismatic variety. I remember thinking it was a little strange, but it beat sitting around the house. And if you made it through the service, you were often treated to lunch. Fast food was the lure.

From rolling in the spirit and faith healings to the smell of French fries and grilled onion, I was cool with the routine and didn't ask any questions. That is, until I went to a Sunday school class with a new teacher. She was an older woman, who taught us all about hell, with an enthusiasm that is rarely seen outside of Disney villains. I

---

[2] I routinely refer to things from my childhood as "lost in the fire." I say that as code for "my parents didn't keep those things" or "we have three pictures of me from the crib to fourth grade." When I first referenced losing things in the fire on Facebook, my sister contacted me to see if everything was cool and to ask if she was forgetting something.

may have been young, but this didn't seem cool. And so, I was out. At least I mentally checked out. As long as girls came to youth groups and I got to go on excursions with "pity for the poor kid" funds, I would stay physically within the walls of a church.

I was no saint, but the message of "be good or else" seemed scary. It was the first time I thought through the implications of what I thought Christianity was. I thought that this "good or else" was bullshit. So I figured I could either live with the scary proposition of "good or else," or else I could choose not to believe, live a happy life, and then become fertilizer. If I chose not to believe, there was no punishment, just death. And even if there was an afterlife, it was a long way off, so I might as well claim ignorance for as long as possible. I thought this through. I remember sitting on my bed thinking through the implications. I was an anti-Pascal by the third grade.

Wherever I was, I must have worn something on my face that told people I needed something; I would be invited to go to the water-parks and miniature golf for free. Later, I learned about summer camp. I had thought it was an all-summer event that was basically an extension of school except the camp counselors were younger than our teachers. Everything I thought I knew about summer camp I learned from *Poison Ivy* with Nancy McKeon (Jo from *The Facts of Life*), and Michael J. Fox (Alex P. Keaton from *Family Ties*). They were counselors at one of those summer-long camps with hijinks and rival camps and allusions to losing your virginity.

The idea of camp was like a dream for a kid who didn't go on vacations and wasn't fond of sticking around the house. There were girls and a pool and late nights around a campfire. I would be ashamed to think of the number of times I used the minor isolation of the mountains and the emotion of late nights with little sleep to endear girls to me. I would feign spiritual sincerity, only to later joke about the middle-aged guy with a tucked in t-shirt and a prodigious gut, lapping over the waist of his cargo shorts. I would be ambivalent about the worship leader that was trying to be a mix between Bob Dylan and Bono. He would be good for whipping up emotions and then an easy target for jokes after he repeated the fourth chorus with his eyes closed, singing the harmonies, and sing-talking made-up lines. By accepting the emotional state he conjured and then using it against him in jokes when it got too uncomfortable, I could seem both pious and a little dangerous.[3] Christian summer camp was a sexually charged hotbed for short relationships, cafeteria-style baked pizza (cut into squares), and kids promising that they would stop whatever naughty behavior they were engaged in once they got saved (or rededicated their lives to the Lord). There was a lot of promising at camp. I saw those kids the week after camp and knew it was all a show. Not to mention what happened behind cabins and in dark corners of the campground after the campfire. It may have been the case, perhaps in hyperbole, that as one nineteenth-century critic of revival camps suggested, "more souls may have been conceived on those evenings than saved."

One more thing about evangelical summer camp: there were always twins. I saw my fair share at these camps and "dated" at least one twin, and another set of twins I camp-dated both, unintentionally. I believe one was Monday, Tuesday, Wednesday, and the other was Thursday when she realized I camp-dated her sister the other days. It was a big misunderstanding. I had arts and crafts with one and outdoor activities with the other, and I couldn't tell them apart. With some twins, one looks like the dial was turned ever so slightly and they came out with a slightly wonky eye or bad teeth. These two Nordic girls with a penchant for shorter, insecure rebels who made fun of camp were identical, at least from across the fire pit semicircle. So on Wednesday night, I locked eyes with the one I thought I was with. It was her sister. She enjoyed my dumb pantomime jokes about the Dylan-esque song leader and the student testimonies. We hung out later and sneaked off behind the cabins. I was always too nervous to make any kind of move, so we usually held hands and kissed and mostly just hugged awkwardly for long periods of time. At any rate, the next morning at breakfast I got a jug of orange juice poured over my head as I ate. I liked the girls-at-church-who-like-the-outsider thing, but I realized that they eventually came to dig the dudes that got into it all and cried and sang with their eyes closed.

Meanwhile, substances were calling. I didn't have a curfew anymore, and so I could just spend the nights walking around town, sitting at various restaurants. (This was before coffee shops; loitering in the suburbs was much harder then.) We didn't have pagers or cell

---

[3] Dangerous by middle-class, evangelical standards.

phones yet, so I would call various friends and occasionally someone with a car would pick me up. I didn't have the fervor in me to become a junkie or drunk in my midteens. I was often told at school I was lazy and unmotivated. Check and double check.

I started hanging around the church again. It was easy to get a ride since my sister went, so I hung out occasionally and found that while being the "outsider" on the "inside" was cool, being the "kind of weird and certainly not-one-of-us" outsiders got you some attention.

Evangelical kids love safe and tame bad kids. We get their nerves a little rattled but not that badly. And if they are ever going to meet a person outside the church with "rebellious" streaks, we serve as practice targets for evangelism.

Chapter 6

A Movie Script Ending

Or, How I Quit or Was Politely Dismissed from Hollywood

A Soundtrack for Reading

1. A Movie Script Ending—Death Cab For Cutie

2. Elevate Me Later—Pavement

3. Los Angeles—Frank Black

4. California—Phantom Planet

5. Drivin' on 9—The Breeders

6. No Room in Frame—Death Cab For Cutie

7. The Night Josh Tillman Came to Our Apartment—Father John Misty

8. The Only Place—Best Coast

9. Whip-Smart—Liz Phair

10. California—Childish Gambino

11. California Love—2Pac

12. Juicy—The Notorious B.I.G.

The highest form of vanity is love of fame.

—George Santayana

I don't want to suggest that all pastors or religious leaders are nar-cissists. I admit, starting a chapter of a book with that caveat might suggest is exactly what I am going to do.

But I'm not. Stay with me.

I think almost everyone is a narcissist. Maybe in different ways, and not always according to the clinical definition, but the stuff we are most interested in usually involves ourselves, our well-being, and our public reputation. We're just bent that way. Maybe pastors are less narcissistic than the average person, because they have dedi-cated their lives to a higher cause. Because they have done this, they are also under tighter scrutiny. So a few bad examples have a way of ruining the reputation for the whole lot of them. I get that.

I do want to suggest, however, that actors are almost always, and by necessity, narcissists. At one point, if you are an actor, you made the determination that you had something that others didn't and that people would pay to see that something. Occasionally, actors have more noble reasons than others. Some classically trained thespians, like Ian McKellen or Ben Kingsley, genuinely seem to be in it for the artistic expression. Others may be trying to find a way to make a living for their families in foreign lands. But then there is everyone else.

What is curious to me about these two professions—actor and pastor—is the curious number of people I have known who have been serious about a career in both acting and the church at various points in their lives, at least in Southern California. I have known five people who have played with both the pulpit and the silver screen as their way of being somebody important. And I only point this out because, when I mention that I've known five people in this category, I'm one of those five.

I will suspend all my judgment of those whose motives I can-not know. But I'll break the seal on my own files. A full account of my life in Hollywood or my brief career arc leading to a life in the church is neither necessary nor as interesting as I might think. But both deserve attention, and both are intricately, and embarrassingly, tied up together with this story.

Permit me to pick up the story somewhere near the end of my illustrious career in Hollywood, as a bit part player, fresh-faced spokesperson, and smiling face for advertisements and television shows.

In 1996, I was in a fairly prominent magazine ad, which was all over the Spanish-language newspaper *La Opinión*. I was the valet opening the door of some car. I was looking friendly as hell, suggesting that you would deserve really good service or receive really good service if you either drove this car or went to this restaurant.

As an actor, I had higher-profile work, but the print job for *La Opinión* always sticks out. I got the call from my agent a few days before the shoot. I needed to be in downtown LA, in front of a restaurant at 4 am, on a weekday. I was pissed off because my car was especially cold and I hated going to these things, then driving back in time for school and having to fill out all the underage attendance paperwork. And this photo shoot wasn't getting me paid much. I was sick of doing this crap work that didn't make for cool stories once I got back to school. What's more, the work didn't come with any residuals. I wasn't ready to give up on my dream of acting, or perhaps, it was my dream of doing little work while being rich and popular.

On my way back from the shoot, I decided to take a freeway with a number I had not encountered before. I have no internal compass, and despite living on a coast, I can't tell directions for shit. But I went in a direction that seemed the opposite of home.

I wanted to feel like I was having an epiphany. I wanted to manufacture some kind of "moment" for myself. I was dramatic. I wanted everything to have "moments" and "epiphanies" and things of great cosmic significance. Most of the time, these moments and epiphanies didn't happen. So I created them. Those moments involved me driving in an alien direction for a long while.

This was prior to GPS, and I only had a Thomas Guide, an old-timey map with a lot of pages. I didn't have an ATM card. If I got lost, I was out of luck. I would have to find a payphone and have money to use it. And have someone to call. I never thought through details as much as I should have.

But I had a plan.

I ended up in a desert-like part of the state. It wasn't well-zoned or gentrified. And this was before the coffee shop craze that provided an excuse to sit somewhere for a while, with only a couple bucks. And so, I began what would become a regular occurrence, I made a bed in the back of my car using sweatshirts and jackets and took a nap.

Sleeping in my car would become a staple of either being too drunk to drive home, waiting down the road from my house for my parents to go to bed before I came home, or trying to sleep off the booze before I went to work or church.

I woke up in the late afternoon, popped in a mix tape, and drove toward the sunset. I felt reborn. I was going to do something with my life that was important. Something that involved . . . I can't remember. But I had manufactured a temporary epiphany and had a soundtrack that included Pavement's "Fillmore Jive" and Yo La Tengo's "I Heard You Looking." These are great tracks for solitary driving and trying to develop a kind of cool, distanced, but sincere and pensive take on the state of things.

I remember feeling like I should make a rash decision and live with the consequences. I wanted to take some big step and then figure out where to go from there. I also wanted to stop doing what I was doing in Hollywood, not necessarily on principle, but because I was sick of doing dumb things that took away from my time hanging out with friends and girlfriends. Never had such laziness met with resolve. Unfortunately, nothing monumental happened following that drive, since my laziness trumped my resolve. This became my modus operandi, and thus, the template for the next half of my life was set.

All of this began when I was a fourteen-year-old in 1993. It was the year of the Branch Davidian showdown in Waco, the Bill Clinton presidency, and the debut season of the *Mighty Morphin Power Rangers*. I had spent most of that year sitting on the floor of my bedroom playing *NHLPA Hockey '93* on my Sega Genesis (a victory for my parents, who put a cable television and video game console in my room to ensure I would not bother them). I would turn the sound down on the game and listen to talk radio. I listened to

the various hosts talk about news, sports, and weather on an interrupted loop with the occasional commercials for job training and
things to surprise your significant other with. In other words, they
figured the demographic was dudes trying to salvage relationships
and get jobs. I wasn't their target audience, but I thought what they
did was a pretty good gig. They had a few minutes to bring up a story,
deliver a half-baked idea, and then condescend to callers whose ideas
were only slightly worse than theirs. This is my cynical recollection;
it was probably a harder job, and I thought it was pretty cool.

One night, I decided to call in to a station when they asked for
David Letterman–style top-ten lists. The callers were all bombing,
so I decided to make mine a top three. I tried lowering my voice to
sound older. I told them I was twenty. The call screener laughed.

"Hello, Dan from Irvine. You're on."

What happened then was not unlike the euphoria I felt the first
time I figured out what the eighth graders had been talking about
during PE.

I killed it. Or at least I killed it as much one can kill it on late-
night sports radio call in shows. The hosts were laughing, asking how
old I was, and then going to commercial. One of the hosts told me to
stay on the line. He told me I was funny, and I could call in anytime.

Like an overly eager boy who just got a look from a pretty girl, I
decided to smother the airwaves with calls. Against my better judgment (or any judgment), I called the show back the next evening
with an unsolicited list. I didn't tell the screener I was going to do it.
But I had it ready.

"It's Dan, the kid from Irvine again."

I launched into the list and they laughed. I don't know if it was
as good as the previous night's, but it felt great. To carry the over-
eager boy calling the girl analogy, I was too euphoric to not call in
again the next night. I had these taped; after all, I wanted to prove to
my friends that I was on the radio. I ended up calling in every night
for over a month. The hosts switched time slots, and I would ditch
class to get to the pay phone by the minimart to call (with my own
dimes and with detentions racking up). My old man told me one
evening about some kid that his friends at work were talking about
that had my name and city. He, uncharacteristically, took me out
to a Monday Night Football party at a bar that the radio show was

hosting. He helped me sneak in, and then I was off to the radio booth to sit in on a segment.

I ended up cohosting a show on a Saturday afternoon, but when one of the hosts was hired by a *Hollywood Tonight* type television program, the radio gig was through. I was off to find something that could give me that same rush. Broadcasting? Comedy? For the first time in my life, I had ditched the schoolboy dreams of becoming an astronaut or firefighter and had started to consider how I was going to make a living.

The hosts told me that the best I could do at this point was to write out what I could and find as many opportunities to perform as possible.

I found an ad for a comedy group that was looking to audition kids for an improv troupe. By audition, I later learned they meant "suck you into paying for classes and then putting on a subpar show for parents and siblings when the club was quiet on a Sunday afternoon." However, something broke right for me, and after the audition, they asked if I would join the adult cast. I did pretty well, doing a few scenes, and was asked by the executive director for my agency's contact information. I didn't have an agent. They made sure I did within a few days.

For the next year or so, I found myself doing improvisational comedy, eating Jack in the Box dinners in crowded dressing rooms and in crap clubs, and hanging out with people who seemed like superstars to a fifteen-year-old. They did comedy for a living! These were anything but comedy superstars. A few of them went on to do some television and work with our sister organization that had a good track record of getting comics onto *Saturday Night Live*. But most of them were fucked up. At fifteen, the difference between a twenty-five-year-old and a forty-five-year-old seems negligible. I think that a few of them were in their twenties, but most were likely in their thirties. They ushered me around and sent me on trips to keep me away from their illicit behavior. But since I had been around and partook of hard drugs since I was thirteen, I could see the white residue on the tables and the dilated pupils and manic behavior during the show and know what was going on. I think knowing that this was happening sort of legitimized it all. I had seen a behind-the-scenes type show on *Saturday Night Live* and figured that drugs + comedy = success. I'm not denying that equation now. It's just that it is as likely that anything + comedy = a fucked-up life.

One of the bigger moments for me on my self-envisioned rise to stardom took place at a Wendy's near my house. I ordered my food, and as I pulled up to the cashier . . . holy shit! It was Regina, the best-of-the-best in our group. If she couldn't pull off a career in show business, such that she had to take a job pulling Frosties and flipping ninety-nine-cent square patties, then I was screwed.

My last time working with the group was in August of 1996. I had gone to a camp with some friends (I can't remember where it was or with whom I went) and did not want to try to make it back for our afternoon run-through of an improv/sketch show we were performing that evening. I figured I could get to the club by fourish with plenty of time to jump into the skits and games. I decided that I would just let it be and show up whenever I happened to show up.

The next memory I have is walking into the club, through the back-door, *Goodfellas* style, winding through the kitchen and then through the back of the club. The director was talking with someone when she saw me. She stopped midconversation and turned her beady eyes toward me. I can still envision those eyes that sunk back into a tautly pulled face, framed by jet black hair. She lambasted me. She humiliated me in front of my fellow performers. She told me that I should be fired.

So I lied to her.

I told her that my Aunt Margaret died and that I tried calling the club but no one was picking up, and that I was running out of quarters. Do you realize how much easier it was to lie about such things before cell phones? I think this is something our kids will never understand and it will keep us more skeptical of their excuses.

She was barely placated by my lies, but the show had to go on, and I was in a few of the big pieces, but this made me a martyr to the rest of the troupe.

"Are you sure you can go on tonight?" a few of them asked.

"Yes," I responded, sounding gloomier than I actually was.

I had my head down and then slowly lifted it while brushing a tear from my eye. As they all waited with baited breath to see how the kid would respond, I would say in my most dramatic and devil-may-care voice: "Let's rock this shit [appropriate pause] for Aunt Margaret."

Of course, I had no Aunt Margaret, nor any intention of going forward with this troupe or with any other Saturday night work for that matter. My friends had cars and were hanging out. Curfews came later to my area, and I was in the midst of the great girlfriend bonanza.

I didn't show up to the club the next weekend. I know the director tried calling my house. It was a simpler time; you made up your mind, didn't return the phone call, and moved on to the next fleeting hobby. And yes, the ironic parallels between this and my girlfriends are not lost. Everything was a placeholder for me. I might not be dating my favorite girl, or doing a Cherry Coke ad, or reading lines for *ER*, but I had to do something. I sure as hell wasn't going to sit down and think about things. Later, when I was diagnosed with depression and severe anxiety disorder, this would make sense. Any stopping for reflection could lead to regret and self-doubt. Whether I knew this or not, it turned out to be a fortuitous personal defect in several ways.

I left the comedy club, and broke up with Melissa Lu (see chapter 8). I believed I was on to bigger, and better, and more popular things, although they were extremely superfluous and vain. I probably knew they were superfluous and vain, but I also knew that was the kind of temporary ego stroke and high I needed. I was on television, though working on crap-paying shows for a Japanese company that made shows that needed American scenes to splice into their Japanese monster-battling footage. I was modeling and dating the head cheerleader of my high school. I was a fucking superstar in my own eyes then. Later, I was able to look back and remember the modest nature of my television work, the embarrassment of being photoshopped for various advertisements, and the cheerleader being the medieval-times enthusiast that rented me the prom formal wear made entirely of felt (see chapter 7 for an explanation of the prom formal wear).

MTV and a Car Painted like an Energy Bar

I started to really think I was onto something big when MTV called. This was the era of *The Real World* and *Road Rules*. *The Real World* was arguably the first reality show with crossover appeal, and its first seasons have likely left some kind of mark on many of those who are in their late thirties. The cast was memorable. Eric Niese! Julie! Puck! Pedro! There was the weird rape accusation on an otherwise forgettable second season in LA. MTV decided it would launch various campaigns across greater metropolitan regions, with promotional items to hand out and live events.

I got an audition.

I went into a small office room (not a traditional casting room) with a group of older gentleman and one youngish woman with semiprofessional, semi-punk-rock red hair. She asked me to hold a microphone and pretend to work like a carnival barker getting people to come to the vehicle and register to win prizes by signing up with their address and social security numbers.

I got the job without a callback. Either they were desperate or I was good. Maybe it was a mixture of the two. Within a few weeks, I was given the keys to a new Mustang, the code to a storage unit with the surfboard and other tchotchkes we were giving out, and I began my weekends driving around to local events and malls, attempting to persuade people to give me their social security numbers. We did this for nothing but the chance to win a surfboard or keychain. And people were happy to oblige. They sent me out for the summer of 1996 in a new cherry-red mustang and with a series of models to host local events.

As an awkward teen, this was a dream come true. I was working at the zenith of MTV's second wave of success. *MTV News* was my generation's main news source. We all knew the weekly programming schedule. And *120 Minutes* was enough to satisfy us music snobs, though we secretly liked the Spice Girls. Soon, my local spots were airing on TV, and I gained a reputation around school as the "MTV guy." I think people wanted to make it a bigger deal than even I did, although I didn't stop them from talking me up. Soon, even the Laura Pullmans and Kaycee Tuckers of the world were talking to me. The "back parking lot bros" gave me the what's-up head nod/chin jerk around school. My transformation to popular kid had commenced. I could now be conversational with people. I could now not be awkward in small group settings or at parties. Except none of that actually ended up happening.

Even a big break couldn't get me out of my introverted, nervous shell. That was mental. Sure, I could stand in front of a crowd and be outgoing or funny with no fear. But personal peace alluded me. Fortunately, the girlfriends kept coming. After all, I was a minor local celebrity (with sideburns!) at seventeen.

That school year, I booked a number of commercials and print ad work. MTV called and asked if I would come back the next summer. I had to do it. I had the ego of a giant but the self-esteem of a gnat. With those things, and a quick hit of success and popularity, any betting person would wager that chemicals and addiction were in my near future.

One of the models I worked with, Stacy, called me sometime in the early spring and asked if I wanted to do an under the table, nonunion job, doing promotion for a national company. The pay would be better than MTV (not hard to do considering that they paid very, very little). The hours would be flexible, and the two of us would spend considerable time hanging out on beaches and at local events. I was sold, but I had to keep any knowledge of my nonunion work from my agent. I drove up to southeastern Los Angeles county (neither glamorous nor gritty, just plain) and headed to the address of a company called Boost! What were we doing? Something like the MTV gig, but with about 1/1000 of the prestige. Boost! was a geriatric supplement, also used by patients that had liquid diets. They wanted to break in on the nascent energy bar craze and give out newly packaged geriatric diet bars to a younger crowd. How would they do this? By repackaging the bars, adding an exclamation point, and having young folks work local promotional gigs.

While it felt weird being at the occasional mall for MTV, Boost! was weirder, sending me to parking lots and strip malls. Eventually, I realized that the higher ups at Boost! cared little about tracking our hours. They just wanted all the hip, extreme new geriatric bars for the next generation gone. And so we began to pick the car up in the AM, drop off the bars in my garage or at a friend's house, and then drive around for the rest of the day. It never struck me as odd that Stacy, a rather attractive young woman of about twenty-five, standing at roughly five foot seven with long brown hair, a tan, and a defined face, was working with me regularly, thus giving me high school cred for what I imagine were made-up escapades in the minds of my friends. But it also never struck me as odd that Stacy didn't shave her legs. Is this unusual? My knowledge of the opposite sex was so limited, due to my general fear, that I would take anyone's word on it. Usually, TV was my best instructor, and there were no hairy legs on *Baywatch*.

I should have seen that this woman was deeply troubled. She recently replied to an ad for someone to fix her car on the cheap. He came over, they made out, and he took her car to his "shop" to fix. He left with the car, and she never saw him again. One day, we were near my apartment, and she said she needed to use the restroom. So we stopped, and she spent a good fifteen minutes crying in the bathroom.

Danger! Eject! Get out!

She kept telling me about the trials of her rough childhood and her financial woes. We ended up at the garage where we were supposed to drop off the car and talked for a while. Actually, she talked and I nodded sympathetically. The rest is a blur, but whatever happened next was physical and awkward and not remotely intimate. It happened in a storage center in southeast LA, in the back of a Ford Explorer painted like a Boost! Bar.

The following Saturday, I drove up early to the place where we picked up the Boost!-mobile and left a note on the front seat saying that I needed to quit. I was usually overly verbose in my notes and probably made up a story about a family illness or a move or some kind. I could break up situations with girls, quit jobs, and do all numbers of things irresponsible and deceitful with aplomb. I supposed this was something like a special power. Granted, I was ashamed of it, but I was more afraid of confrontation than my own bad behavior.

I kept at my regular audition work and ended up making some money working on a variety of shows that were all filmed in a forest area outside of Los Angeles. It was a set for a number of Japanese shows that made a jump to America: *Might Morphin Power Rangers*, *Big Bad Beetleborgs*, and their various spin offs. I would regularly get called to be something like "hiker #2" or "lunch yard bully." All the action scenes were already filmed with the Japanese actors, so we had to do all the stuff that wasn't dubbed. It would involve me getting to a trailer at some ungodly hour in the morning and then reading sides (small scripts with limited and banal dialogue) and then sitting in a makeup chair or with wardrobe as they made me out to be another character on one of the shows they were filming that day. It was lame, but I figured I was headed in the right direction. And when MTV called with an audition for a regular lead role on an evening teen soap opera, I would be ready. I went to the swank LA studios, not the little satellite offices I had done the promo hosting work out of. They faxed me sides with extended dialogue and had me read it with various people. They took pictures of me with various outfits and wanted to test my chemistry with other actors. I returned for two callbacks and assumed I was ready to make the final cut.

On a warm and bright summer afternoon in 1999, I was with my friends Kyle and Beth Anne, and we decided it was a good day for the beach. We were all in town that day (they were both attending college in LA), and we had been hanging out a good bit. None of us had plans, so we decided to head off to spend the day at the beach, an outdoor shopping center, and eventually the Coco's where we regularly ended our evenings. I remember feeling really relaxed, a rarity for me at any stage in life, but especially as the high school/college transition was happening and I was prone to melancholy and anxiety attacks. All was going to be well. It was sunny, and these friends would end up being both one of my best friends and my wife.

And then I got a page. I went to a pay phone and called the number. It was my agency telling me I needed to get to LA to meet with the producers of *Undressed* for some screen tests.

I have no recollection as to what went through my brain when I calmly told my agent, "I can't make it, sorry."

"This is really important. We can probably book this today; you need to be there," my agent, Jackie, replied.

"Yeah . . . I can't . . . sorry," I replied with laconic disinterest.

"I don't think you realize how important this is. You need to be there this afternoon. What time can you be there?"

"Today isn't going to work. Sorry. Things are busy," I replied with a mix of stoicism and eagerness to get back with my friends to spend a day doing nothing around the beach.

"Maybe, Daniel, you need to rethink your commitment to this agency and to your career," Jackie told me sternly.

"Okay."

I hung up the phone and went back to Kyle and Beth Anne. I don't know what I told them. I felt bad for being lazy but had learned to quell my angst over my laziness as a survival mechanism.

I never spoke with my agency again. A few residual checks came in, but I never even considered going back. Part resolve to do something else, part laziness.

I was asked, within the week, to give a talk at a youth gathering, and I decided I would talk about not going on the callback with MTV. Never underestimate the connection between drama and moral testimony. I told the kids that I had made the decision because of a moral stand. I told them that Jesus wouldn't want me on that show, and so I had to stand up for my faith and was promptly persecuted by my agency for refusing to do work that interfered with my conscience. It was a winning talk. I feel bad that I didn't really feel bad about making that part up. The gist of it was true; I was now working in a church instead of in Hollywood. It came on the heels of me not going to a callback for a racy nighttime soap on MTV. I probably convinced myself that it was an actual religious and moral stance. Looking back, I know it was much more about hating the drive to LA, not having air conditioning, and the prospect of missing out on hanging out with my friends.

My friend Jeff, who went from troubled kid, to acting, to academia and now cohosts a podcast with me, also had a fork in the road decision to make when he had to confront his values and his decision to stay in acting. He first got interested in Hollywood after he got to go to NBC studios to be a contestant on teen week for the game show *Scrabble*. After getting an agent, he was getting more lucrative roles like a Cherry Coke commercial (national residuals!) and was on the short list for role of Zack Morris on *Saved by the Bell*. He actually quit acting for religious reasons. He refused to be in the adaptation of Stephen King's *IT*, a PSA for AIDS (why that was a moral stance befuddles me), and anything with sex in it. Oh, and he didn't want to do anything connected to Universal Studios, which his church was boycotting in response to *The Last Temptation of Christ*.

I played it the exact opposite way. I left, not by way of a moral stand, but out of laziness, which I then parlayed into a great message about morality and conviction, which was almost completely fabricated. MTV was casting for its middling successful late-night teen drama *Undressed*. I had been called up to audition and made two callbacks. I remember driving home one late morning, drowsy, in my green Volkswagen bug, and it hit me. "Holy shit! I'm going to make this jump to TV." I was trying to stay awake while driving in traffic. (Side note: If I die young from some kind of tragedy, it is going to involve falling asleep while driving. Side note to that side note: it's creepy to publish something like that, and it will make this part of the book really awkward if that happens. Sorry.)

I had already signed a rental agreement for a place up in LA for the coming fall, to live with Kyle and our friend Matt, since they would be at UCLA and I would be close to auditions. But now I was out of the acting business. So I spent that fall in our LA apartment (which looked remarkably like a worn-down version of Melrose Place) loafing in the apartment, in a bathrobe, smoking, and drinking coffee. Kyle and Matt would get up and go to school, and I would get up late, have a smoke in bed while reading something (I had actually started reading voraciously at this point), and then move to the couch and watch midday television with black coffee, a pack of Lucky Strikes, and zero ambition. It was delightful.

Don't underestimate how wonderful it is to smoke inside your own place. It's not good for your heath, of course. It's disgusting, and gives everything the stale scent of smoke. But it is really convenient, and made me feel grown up as a nineteen-year-old. I lived for the first month or so on residual checks from acting. I would sit on the couch, in my bathrobe, until the sun made its way across the sky and started to get in my eyes. Rather than move or close the curtain, I took that as my cue to take an early afternoon nap. I was, however, reading as much as I could with a newfound interest. This, of course, would augur things to come. Prior to that time, I had maybe read three books cover-to-cover in my life. Now reading was becoming my thing.

Unfortunately, I turned out to be a lousy roommate. I couldn't stand the sound of eating or clanking of bowls. I was going through a pretty bad bout of depression, and my answer to that was to keep feeding the silent, black beast of despair. Much to the chagrin of Kyle and Matt, I listened to Sunny Day Real Estate and Liz Phair on repeat (dig "Canary" on her *Exile in Guyville* album). My pre-Lebowski version of the Dude could only last so long. I began to run out of money, so I got a job at a coffee shop. I worked there for about a week when a homeless dude—a very large homeless dude—walked into the store with nothing but an American flag draped around his waist and a Super Soaker water gun. He started spraying the gun, and when I thought I should tell the gentleman that this was against our policy, he came up to the pastry case and started pounding the plastic water gun on it, telling me he was going to kill me. I make it a policy not to take death threats from large homeless men wearing a sarong made out of Old Glory very seriously. So I went to the manager in the back and told him there was a problem on the floor. I took my lunch break and headed home. I decided I wouldn't work there anymore. I found that I could leave jobs with the same detachment with which I broke up with girls. I just stopped showing up and calling. They got the message, and I was free to move on.

It was around this time that I found religion.

I got a small job at the church back home, to lead the middle schoolers on Wednesday nights. So I commuted, routinely left a mess at the apartment, and would drive home on Wednesday nights, trying not to fall asleep in my car. I had foolishly sold my bug to buy a Honda CR-X, which was automatic, quieter, and faster and thus lulled me into sleep much more easily. My relationship with my roommates deteriorated. Like an unhappy couple thinking that a new baby will fix their relationship, we decided to adopt a puppy. It did not go well. When we left the apartment for Christmas break and decided to let the dog stay with bowls of water and food lined against the walls, we should have realized that we weren't responsible enough to care for an animal. We came back to our apartment with our apartment torn to shreds and an unhappy dog. (We called him Ira after the lead singer of Yo La Tengo.) We gave the puppy away, and I let a friend take over my part of the lease.

I moved back to Orange County to live in my parents' apartment. I started working at a coffee shop as well as at the church and was eventually told that I would be in line to take over the junior high group altogether, if I wanted to commit to staying in the area. I thought I should go to college and thought that moving away would give me a new lease on life. But I had dropped out of junior college and had no hope of getting into the state university in town.

It was during this time that I also took a job offer to lead a youth group at a church where the pastor, Tom Gastil, who was instrumental in my conversion to Christianity, was now the head pastor. This story does not end well. But it was this pastor who initially took me under his wing as a father figure, took me to Rams practices at the local college, and made a point of highlighting my work in comedy and on the radio.

I can't overestimate this man's influence on my early life. He did not try to convince me to join his religious tribe with clever arguments or a heavy hand. There was something that made him different. I believe that he took an interest in me as a human. He loved a messed up kid in a way that I had not experienced. I was not looking to religion as a crutch. In fact, to paraphrase C. S. Lewis, if I were to pick a religion, it wouldn't be Christianity. While the message is, when done well, all about grace and forgiveness and love, it is still a commitment both to some strange ideas and also to a complete reordering of my life. I quit drinking for a season and stopped using illegal substances.

My work at the church was uneventful. Like any workplace, I had run-ins with various people and even came to disagree on a few rather subtle things with Tom. I realized that I really liked teaching and talking about important topics. I realized that I could love people, however imperfectly, in a way that might mean something to other broken people. But I wasn't made for a position in the church. When a pastor is a real pastor who has devoted his or her life to the care of souls, it is a noble calling. I really wanted to teach and be left alone. I wasn't interested in playing games or singing melodramatic worship songs on my guitar. So I would eventually leave the church, the summer after I graduated from college, and did so by tendering my resignation and then leaving through the back door. But sometime during my tenure at this church, I would meet the Brothwells: Don, Elizabeth, and their three sons. Their friendship, mentoring, and continued advice are a major part of my life. I want to keep this story as streamlined as possible—but if we ever meet, ask me about them.

Back in my days at the previous church, the junior high leader, from whom I was presumed to take over when he jumped up to the high school position, encouraged me to look at the little college hidden up in the hills, near many of my friends and only a stone's throw from my old high school. This little college had apparently been around for some time but didn't do a very good job promoting itself. I applied and met with an older lady at the college to explain my lack of junior college units (I only had six after a year and a half) and to explain to her that I had gone to the top-notch local high school and that I had scored a 1490 on the SATs. This little college was Concordia University, the place that would impact my life more than any institution. It became the cradle of my nascent academic career and the crucible where almost every major decision I would make for the next seventeen years took place. It was there that I met an old irascible theology professor who, despite his reputation among some as curmudgeonly, would routinely be moved to tears in lectures and would hire me to keep his academic affairs in order. There, I would take a class on Hemingway from a tall and slightly awkward professor who would later become my boss and almost fire me for tweeting about a commencement address and my love of "fucking raisins." At Concordia, not only did I end up marrying Beth Anne, but I learned a good deal about training my mind and thought I might make a career out of teaching. I couldn't be certain, because my laziness always looked for the path of least resistance, but at least I considered it. I also had a last minute substitute as an Old Testament professor. He was a young kid fresh out of Oxford, who had also graduated from Concordia a few years back. He was most certainly not an Old Testament scholar, but as I came to learn, you can pretend to know just about anything for a semester. This young overachiever was a baby-faced and wet-behind-the-ears Jeff Mallinson.

He would spend most of the time rushing through the required material to then talk about wild theories regarding ziggurats and aliens. He would skip passages in Deuteronomy in order read from the book of Ecclesiastes and talk about staring down meaningless- ness. He engaged us (or at least me) with his breezy lecture style that was prone to tangents and pop-culture references. We talked after class one day about our mutual love of *No Depression*–style indie country rock bands. We would meet for drinks at a local bar occasionally (he was only five years older than I was), and he told me that I should consider applying to a university for a graduate degree. Despite being a theology major myself, he told me that my best chance was to bridge into a different field (I chose history) if I wanted to be employed. He suggested the University of St. Andrews in Scotland or Oxford, where he had studied. I applied to both and was accepted by both. I received e-mails from the head of school at St. Andrews, and this was coupled with a trip to Oxford, where I was accosted by a homeless man. (My fear of the homeless is really an underappreciated part of my life; perhaps I should engage this in a later book.) I decided St. Andrews was the school for me, and with the same restless and unplanned urge with which I quit acting, got engaged, and later quit drinking, I jumped into graduate school. Hollywood would have to wait.

All of this is important for me to recollect as it pulls together disparate stories and periods in my life that all had to do with professional acting and comedy. This section has connected experiences from junior high to graduate school. There is no way to tell my story in a completely linear fashion. I never lived a strictly linear life. It is important to remember that all the following chapters took place with this chapter's narrative as the backdrop. As we get uncomfortable and talk about my ex-girlfriends, please keep in mind this picture of me in these past chapters. I was the kid making the bad decisions, trying to gain favor with other troubled kids. I was the kid working in Hollywood and in comedy clubs and for MTV trying to have fun, make money, impress girls, and somehow or other, to matter.

CHAPTER 7

Young Adult Friction

Or, Awkward Teenage Dating and Why I'm Glad I Don't Have Daughters

A Soundtrack for Reading

1. Young Adult Friction—The Pains of Being Pure at Heart

2. Please Let That Be You—The Rentals

3. Crazy for You—Best Coast

4. I Am Trying to Break Your Heart—Wilco

5. Don't Look Back in Anger—Oasis

6. Boys Don't Cry—The Cure

7. This Charming Man—The Smiths

8. No One Else—Weezer

9. I'm Stealin' to Be Your One in a Million—The Lassie Foundation

10. Why Won't They Talk to Me?—Tame Impala

11. Theme for a Pretty Girl That Makes You Believe God Exists—Eels

12. Everything I Try to Do, Nothing Seems to Turn Out Right—The Decemberists

> *He found something that he wanted, had always wanted*
> *and always would want—not to be admired, as he had*
> *feared; not to be loved, as he had made himself believe;*
> *but to be necessary to people, to be indispensable.*
>
> —F. Scott Fitzgerald

The night of the prom, I ended up asleep on her sofa. I was alone. A movie had finished, and the sleep icon on my computer bounced slowly around the four corners of the dark screen. Everyone had said their farewells and had their romantic walks toward their cars. Meanwhile, I had restless dreams about the dance. I had failed terribly to impress the opposite sex and spent awkward time alone on the dance floor, during midtempo power ballads. I had gotten only so far as to hold my date's hand. On all accounts, it was a failure.

As I slept, I was sweating through my felt black onesie, and the faux leather boots clung to my genetically cursed wide feet like a vise grip.

One hundred percent true.

A felt fucking onesie and faux-leather boots. The gal who picked this outfit for a prom was a cheerleader and generally considered among the most attractive girls at school. I made a fool of myself for someone with social capital and clout. I ended up looking like a leftover extra from Medieval Times. It was a microcosm of my relationship with the opposite sex throughout my adolescence.

Let me tell you the story of how I managed to have nineteen girlfriends in six years, all of whom ended up with their own version of waking up and sweating in boots fit for a Goth Ronald McDonald. These are stories we all retell because they involve the thrill of the chase and the humiliation brought on by the social mores and traditions, revolving around high school dances and pep rallies.[1] These dances were a primary motivator for securing girlfriends and were an excuse to point out to others the kind of social status you had. A rough count of the number of dances I went to in the last two years of

---

[1] Can we get behind the idea that school dances are absolutely absurd? I am sure that by the time my sons get to high school, they will have come up with a reason to discontinue them after one results in a beating, a murder, or too many children conceived the night of. If aliens came to observe our culture, I am convinced that the dance slapped onto a public institution for mandatory learning would strike them as absurd.

high school is sixteen. Holy hell, that's a lot of pressure. Fortunately, I had dates. Unfortunately, I was utterly incapable of anything as suave as *Beverly Hills 90210*'s Dylan, who procured a hotel room for an after party. Many high school dances end up in hotels or car backseats, places conducive to losing one's virginity and initiating a scandalous pregnancy. Lucky for me, my stories don't end up there. They are tame. And humiliating. And meaningless. And they answer many questions.

I was dating the idea of a girl, rather than the actual person who happened to be standing next to me in the dance picture. I genuinely liked these girls. But I liked the idea of them more. The idea of a girlfriend could be put on like a coat but also could be shed like unnecessary skin. They served a purpose: my purpose. These weren't fantasy relationships. They involved two people, one of which happened to be a self-centered asshole. I became emotionally entangled with them because, on some level, they decided that they would tangle with me. I would get their attention and try to grab it all for myself. I would smother them for brief bouts (when it suited me), meanwhile waiting for them to try to grab my attention and affection back.

My approach to dating simultaneously involved both the most and also least narcissistic impulses in my personality. I liked the girls because they liked me. In other words, the quality I liked best about them was the fact that they liked me. I was so in love with myself that love of me was the number one requirement of a girlfriend. At the same time, dating was like self-flagellation in that I clung onto these girls like a parasite, knowing that I couldn't be anybody without somebody validating me, by giving me all their attention. They served as the host, and I was desperately syphoning everything I could from them, until they flicked me off.

Being a world-class asshole, I would try to time their flicking with my jumping. At worst, I could claim it was a mutual break up, and at best, I could come out relatively unscathed and leave girl *x* for girl *y* (thereby showing girl *y* how much she meant to me by my abandonment of girl *x*). I was a fucking Fonzie at this stuff. I felt bad about the way I maneuvered around girls to set up the budding relationships as old ones were winding down. I had an elaborately constructed method of presenting myself as naïve and vulnerable, with a certain amount of social capital. I was the cool but mysterious new guy/actor with early facial hair (expressed in long sideburns, which seemed to work).

I usually can't pin down exactly when I decided to jump from one relationship to the next or if there was any definitive conversation that ended the relationship. I just moved on when it felt right and when a new host presented herself. I was never angry at the girl when I moved on. It's just that I was no longer enamored of the idea of her. In retrospect, my lack of real emotion and intimacy is obvious, since only two relationships had much of an effect on me after the fact. I was mostly interested in them as a sign of my own security and a reflection of my own self-worth.

If you are reading this thinking you have found the inner monologue of one of the most colossal self-indulgent objectifying pricks you've ever come across, I can't do anything to change your mind. And I probably agree with you. But let me defend myself. Kind of.

I never had sex with any of these girls, I think, but there is an asterisk coming. I wouldn't have minded, but I knew that once you took that step, you probably had to stick around awhile. Plus, I was a virgin and had the fear of pregnancy, STDs, and AIDS (especially in the '90s) drilled into me by too many angry PE coaches and home room speeches. I was shown health videos akin to *Reefer Madness* and Red Scare propaganda films, filled with dire warnings of what sex could do to you. It was enough to make me afraid to let my penis make my decisions. So I decided to think with my inflated ego instead.

There were intense make out sessions in the backs of various cars in the backs of poorly lit apartment complex parking lots, but that was it. So I never slept with any of them. Score one for chivalry.

I don't know if there was any one point where I went from a form of adolescent puppy love to a more deeply emotional and relatively mature relationship. I have tried to catalog girls based on my grade, or if I was driving, or if we French kissed or not. A chronological approach doesn't work. I thought I could identify a mature relationship with a girl by determining whether we had a song. From "More than Words" by Extreme, through mix tapes that highlighted mature taste (how many of you had covers of "Big Star" by obscure indie darlings on your list?), to the absurd (ironically placed tokens of affection such as "The Lady in Red" by Chris De Burgh). I wasn't sure how to go about telling these little stories that illustrate a level of alienation and manic obsession, and so I fell back on an old trope: the top-ten list.

It is almost embarrassing how many of the formative stories from my youth involve my goofy infatuation or saccharine gestures of chivalry and cringeworthy awkwardness with girls. I was obsessed with the idea of dating girls. As I mentioned, these were not sexual relationships. I want to take a quick moment and suggest that when we move from chaste to "sexually active" on the doctor's checkup list, we are missing a crucial intermediate step: teenage fumbling.

Teenage Fumbling

A regular person, when they decide to move in for a kiss, looks at the person, slightly tilts their head and then slowly—but with confidence—moves toward the other person's face. It sounds aggressive, but we usually think it is romantic, so long as it is reciprocated. Teenage fumbling, rather than an assertive tilt and glide/dart, involves inching closer and closer to the person, but not making eye contact to scare them off. You might start bravely with a big hug and then keep your face planted on them, chin to clavicle, and start to slowly move your face in the direction of theirs. They may or may not start wrapping their own face and neck in your direction. An advanced teenage fumbler will attempt a small kiss on the cheek or earlobe. But usually, when we start, we just smash our necks and chins and faces together until a kiss has been initiated.

Teenage fumbling is uncertain about what to do with the hands. If the heads are close in proximity, or some sort of kissing has commenced, the hands become like wet noodles. Regular teenage awkwardness has a kind of choreographed hand movement, wherein a chess game is played with advances and retreats. In various cultures, countries, and times, there have been both safe zones and also areas of extreme risk. Depending on where you are in the maturation process, you might find yourself with different borders at different times with different levels of risk. All of this is daunting and can be like a medieval map of Germany (vaguely defined and perpetually shifting).

If you are reading this and what I'm saying sounds foreign, congratulations. You avoided the pitfalls of the emotional and sexual insecurities that led to teenage fumbling. You probably had the confidence to move beyond teenage fumbling. Or you may have moved straight into teenage everything-but-sex, or you slowed down and went back to a kind of awkward embracing that has a sweet and innocent charm (though one you would nonetheless not want your parents to find you in).

In sex ed we were told about something called "heavy petting." This is not a word anyone understands or actually uses. I believe a group of fortysomethings who ended up working in the education division of the State Department of Health tried talking about sexual activity and went back to their own high school experiences and tried to explain to the others in gentle and reserved language what they think the "kids are doing these days." The mishmash of high school sexual experiences by people who end up working in the State Department of Health—Education Division ends up becoming "heavy petting," but we all know that could mean everything from mutual masturbation, to teenage fumbling, to actual grown-up sex.

Girls, Girls, Girls

I would ask that you look at these stories as you would a pointillist painting. Think of the only pointillist you know: Georges Seurat, the nineteenth-century French artist who painted that famous piece in which people are at a park, on the bank of a river. It is composed with small dots of color, and you only see the whole picture when you step back. Taken by itself, this chapter might appear to be about a dude going through ex-girlfriends and trying to process what went wrong. (See, for example, *High Fidelity* by Nick Hornby and the really good movie adaption starring John Cusack. I wish I could be Rob, the main character, and he is pretty pathetic.)

Several people, upon hearing about this book, were baffled as to how a chapter like this would fit in, and another group only wanted me to compile these stories. Indeed, there is an annoying phenomenon in which stories include romantic elements that are unnecessary and detract from the overall style and culture of a work. Most often, we see this when movies bring in love interests to make the film broadly appealing and suitable for a date night. Here's a list of movies that do not need the drama to be interrupted by the relationship or relationship clouded with unnecessary drama:

5. *Pearl Harbor*: it's a garbage movie on all accounts. The love scenes are especially out of place and tedious. Japan bombed America. In real life! This is dramatic enough. *Saving Private Ryan* didn't need romance.

4. *Say Anything*: Did we need to know about the guy who played the dad on *Frasier* and his defrauding of people at the senior community he owned? Let me watch more the awkwardness of Cusack moving Ione Skye out of the way of broken glass on their walk home or Skye's giving Cusack a pen as a sign of affection and closure. I want to see them work it out from the party to the airplane. Everything else needs to go.

3. Every *Die Hard*: I would pay twenty-five bucks on the black market for a copy of each of those movies with the extraneous romantic subplots edited out.

2. *Face-Off*: This was the most absurd movie made during my lifetime. Somehow, John Travolta and Nicholas Cage swap actual faces to work as the other, and the most unbelievable part is that their wives have no idea. Joan Ryan's character, an affectionate but concerned wife, not only gets in the way of the watchable train wreck of the plot line involving a complete transformation of a pudgy Travolta trying to thwart an emaciated Nick Cage and his plan to blow stuff up. Come to think of it, most Cage movies could ditch the romance. *Con Air*? *Gone in Sixty Seconds*? *Ghost Rider*? *National Treasure*? None of them need romance. I need Cage doing Cage-like things and stuff going fast or blowing up.

1. *Star Wars: Attack of the Clones*: This movie seems like a sitting duck, but I actually liked most of it. This is a movie about one of the most curious and foundational events in the galaxy soon to be inhabited by Luke, Han, Leia, and Chewie. They decided to keep Natalie Portman but went

from Anakin as little kid to a brooding young adult by moving to Hayden Christensen. Portman was romantically involved with a kid she showed a little too much affection for. OK, now he's grown up. Cut all of the picnic, rolling around, and romantic bits. Padme exists to give us the twins. I want more clone wars and less relationship that ends up with her dying and Anakin moving to the Dark Side.

So is my story a book about recovery or relationships? Addiction or self-interested relationships? Yes.

Both.

There is a strong connection between both. After all, addictive substances and romantic relationships tickle the same part of the brain. Throughout my teenage years, I was terrified of any kind of relationship but certain that I needed someone to fill an emotional void by having "obligation" to care about what I was doing. I needed to either drink away or date away my deep sense that I lacked human connection. I suspect many relationships are based on this. One of the major theses of this book is that the addict is always an addict and is "cured" not by sobriety but by intimacy. For this, a real human connection must be formed.

I had no prior experience with real human connections, so once again, I was taught about this phenomenon by the all-seeing eye of television. Especially melodramatic teen shows. I'm not ashamed to admit that I can recount frighteningly specific details about *Saved by the Bell* and *Beverly Hills, 90210*. I needed a Kelly (Kapowski or Taylor) or at least a Violet Bickerstaff or Donna Marten (both played by Tori Spelling) to which I could pin my socially conscious character. But I lacked the cool confidence of Dylan or Slater. And I couldn't quite get the slightly too-clever-but-cute Brandon or Zack. I was no Screech or early David Martin. But I wanted to be an amalgamation of them all. Unfortunately, I ended up with a puddle of confusion and disappointment.

To try to detach myself, somewhat, from the strange, arduous, and self-satisfying nature of looking at past relationships, I have taken this chapter and broken it down systematically. So the chapter will be laid out like this: I will be counting down my top ten girlfriends, beginning with honorable mentions. I did not share the same kind of relationship with each of these girls. Some were hardly relationships at all; others were serious. The countdown reflects the impact I think they ultimately had on my psyche and on how I viewed the opposite sex.

I don't think I am at fault in the downfall of all these relationships, but I must take the brunt of things in my retelling the story. I could tell you that I believe "girl *x*" was legitimately crazy. I believe that I was justified in breaking off some of the relationships, though doing so by simply ignoring them until they went away was not a chivalric move. Only one girl ever called me out on my bullshit, wouldn't let me get out easy, and made me realize that I didn't want to be the asshole that walked away from problems. She gets her own chapter, as we've been married for more than fifteen years.

It is my goal to be charitable throughout this section, so I deleted the reference to one of the girls "looking like a bleached troll doll." You know, one of those little plastic trolls that you arranged their hair in a kind of vertical point and then shook them until their hair splayed out like the top of a pineapple. This relationship, however, is so hazy in my mind that I can't remember who broke up with whom. It took me a while to remember her name. Nevertheless, she will be left alone.

I do not hold any ill will toward these girls who were sucked into my vortex of crazy, emotional, awkward teen years. Some have remained friends, while others I fear might like to see my head on a pole. I am very grateful that some of them have written footnotes throughout the next chapter.

If any of you are concerned about adult content, have no fear; there is very little sexual interaction in this chapter. It was not because I was a paragon of virginal purity, but rather because I was often too scared to try to have sex. But don't fear: there is plenty of awkward hormone-driven teenage fumbling, puppy love turned strange test case for future girlfriends, and last ditch attempts to continue in ridiculous relationships. Let's start with ten through five.

10. Jennifer

Jennifer was a nice girl. She was also older, attractive, and popular with my friends. She also worked on a ride at a theme park and could recite the script of the entire ride on cue. I remember the first time I saw her. It is one of the only times I remember the precise first time I saw a girl. I was sixteen and filled with nerves, hormones, and anxiety. I was at someone's house, and she was sitting on the staircase below a vaulted ceiling and skylight. When I looked over at her, I saw sunlight through her hair and a giant warm smile and a green and plaid shirt/skirt combination. I froze in my tracks. I was staring, but I don't remember anyone hitting me. This was more than a girl. I didn't think she was real until she asked me to go with her to her school's dance. I was elated. She wore a formal Japanese kimono. I kept her picture with me to show my friends how attractive my girlfriend from another school was.

She was everything I had wanted. Eventually, however, I became so erratic that I couldn't stand anyone asking for my time or attention. I broke up with her by not calling her (I eventually perfected this art). I hid from her in the basement of a church and ended up abandoning my car as I ran out of a side door and down to a record shop, where I spent a few hours waiting for the scene to clear. She got the message, and we never spoke again. Until Facebook. We have shared pleasantries and I learned about her own experience with substance abuse and the redemption possible. She also loved, and still loves, a musical that I think is beyond rubbish. That reason alone should've disqualified any attempt at a relationship.

9. Rebecca

We were always good friends. I thought, and was likely right, that this was a purely platonic relationship. It started as a date, however. She lived two cities over, and I was supposed to pick her up. I think I left to pick her up at about five. By nine, I had called her three times from a payphone trying to get directions. (Note for the kids: pre-GPS, you could just get lost and have no idea where you were until a gang of drugged-out hobos came and beat you up, left you for dead, and took all your possessions off you. Seriously, everyone over thirty-five has a story like this.) The date didn't work out, but we ended up hanging out a good bit. It was a platonic relationship until we started hanging out when she was back from college on the East Coast. The angst and melancholy that overcame so many when they left for school, and then visited for the first couple times, caused a lot of emotional confusion and havoc (see numbers eight, four, two, and one). One evening, over a cup of coffee, she asked why we had never made out. Challenge accepted! I ended up performing terribly. We had a few sessions of awkward teenage fumbling, one during a crucial interim in a significant relationship with someone else. We didn't talk for almost a decade. Gladly, we have been in touch, and as it has been with so many of these women, she has turned out to be wonderfully adjusted and married despite the residue left on her by me. Metaphorically. A regrettable metaphor. But only a metaphor.

8. Gina

That's right, Gina, you are number eight. I'm going to add you to this list and give you a position, but not one with that much dignity. You see, Gina was at least five years older than me and in college. She had some of that "back from college for the first time" melancholy and befriended a kid just finished with his sophomore year. You like *Beverly Hills, 90210* and Alanis Morissette? Me too. And I'll defend Alanis beyond what some people might because I am insecure and somewhat ashamed of my love of the Canadian songstress. Apparently, Gina didn't get the word that as an attractive college student you don't go resting your head on an impressionable kid. You also don't call them regularly and hang out every day. And you shouldn't write them from college and flirt via snail mail. I don't like thinking about this. Who was I kidding? Who was she kidding? Me.

7. Carly

So I actually dated number ten. I did not date nine or eight. Number seven is hazy. She was a kind of Gal Friday. She loved frozen yogurt. Why has froyo been mentioned in this book more than my parents? I'll write it again: it was huge in the '90s. You won't understand unless you were there. Carly and I had an unspoken sexual tension. Once, while sleeping on the floor with other students on leadership retreat, we embarrassingly and awkwardly moved toward each other like inchworms in our sleeping bags and ended up kissing. We went on dates, even though I was already dating April Anderson. And then we stopped dating and kissing. It was strange how easily we slipped back into a friendship. She later referenced our tryst in my yearbook, taking up a whole page, which should have been for April, so I tried to cover some of the parts up. April already knew (or so I learned when April and I met up twenty years later to discuss this book).

6. Andrea

This was my shortest relationship, and one that could be summed up with the fact that I brought her a Diet Coke, on a tray, during our one afternoon of dating. The story is worth telling.

"You don't kiss?" I asked Gary as he was bragging, in a strange sixth-grade manner, about his escapades with Andrea. And by escapades, he probably meant French kissing and something he called "filling her up," which was not as dirty as it sounds, but rather something he made up, due to a fundamental misunderstanding of basic human anatomy.

"Yeah, I'll prove it," he shot back with his half scowl, half smile.

"All right."

"Let's go then."

"Where?" I did not know what kind of evidence he was planning to produce.

"Get on my pegs." As always, without a bike of my own, I rode on the back pegs of the bike we stole and he kept.

We got to Andrea's house a few blocks away, and he started yelling toward her window.

She came to the window. I remember her wearing some kind of overalls and a patterned shirt that looked like something that Kimmy Gibbler would wear on *Full House*. She squinted, was possibly flattered, and whisper-shouted, "What?"

"Dan doesn't believe we French kiss, come down," Gary said to her in a "Can you believe this guy?" tone.

Holy crap! I only sort of knew what that was but knew it meant something serious. I thought he was going to ask for verification of a subtler sort. My body shuddered and tingled and had all the strange feelings of nerves and hormones and revulsion and wonder that course through a twelve-year-old's body 96 percent of the day.

Andrea came out the front door and told him they couldn't kiss now because her dad was home.

"Just quick, over by the side," he said, as he pointed to the small area between her house and her neighbor's where trash bins were usually kept. This romantic trick worked, partly, as they walked over with Gary wildly waving his arms for me to follow. They kissed, but she pushed him back, presumably as he attempted to add the French component to the encounter.

"See, there." Andrea said to both him and me.

I shook my head with the pursed lips and raised eyebrows of a man whose bluff had just been called. We got back on Gary's bike and road home.

Within a few days, Andrea's friend Jamie summoned me out of the handball line and over by the drinking fountains at school. She told me that Andrea didn't like Gary anymore and wanted to go out with me instead.

"So . . . ," I responded, leaving open an opportunity for her to tell me what to do next.

"Ask her out," she said, as if that was obviously the only option I had.

There were many ways of talking about relationships in the pre- and early-teen years. You could "like" someone or "like-like" someone. You could "meet up" or "go out," but to "go out" wasn't the same thing as "going out." The tense of the verb was important. In past generations, people talked about going "steady" or "going with," but we considered these terms malapropisms of our dumb older siblings and parents.

After recess, I went over by Andrea's desk and awkwardly crouched down next to her.

"Wanna go out?"

By using the ambiguous verb "go out," I stood a better chance at her saying yes. She could interpret it any way she wanted. The next few minutes are blocked out of my memory as I either had a rush of blood to, or from, my head and I probably stared at the carpet, terrified and elated and confused.

That afternoon, she called Gary's house to get ahold of me. He didn't seem to care and nonchalantly handed me the phone.

"Hi," I said, trying to limit the number of words I could embarrass myself with.

"Hey, Dan . . . you want to do something?"

Bingo! See, girls, you are always more mature and straightforward and will help everything if you take small huddled boys filled with nerves and hormones and lead them by the hand.

"Sure, maybe the park . . . do you want a soda?"

"Okay, see you there later."

I sat my pudgy, 5-foot-something frame on the kitchen linoleum, right next to where the phone was. It was my first real date. With Andrea, the girl who kissed in the French style. *I don't know how to kiss*, I thought. What the hell would I have to say? After all, I didn't know anything about her.

"Gary?"

"What?" he shouted from the other room.

"Come with me to the park to meet Andrea?"

"Fine," he responded, as if I just asked if he wanted to share some nachos or watch *Charles in Charge*.

We walked to the park and sat by a eucalyptus tree that was just far enough away from the park, where moms and small children were, and close enough to the curb that we could see when Andrea was coming. As is so often the case, I went shaky and sweaty, and I stuttered.

Gary and Andrea started talking about something. This was a huge relief, since I couldn't speak. Yet this was my "new girlfriend" talking with her old boyfriend, on a date between her and me.

"Do you like Diet Coke?" I blurted out.

"Okay," they both replied in unison.

I had my mission. I had my quest. I would sneak home and grab two cans of Diet Coke from the fridge. But when I got back, I couldn't hand them to both of them in precisely the same manner. That would make me their waiter, not her boyfriend. So I grabbed a floral tray sitting on a shelf. I sprinted back toward the park, and just before I got to the eucalyptus tree, I put Gary's can in my pocket and placed Andrea's Diet Coke on the tray. I served it to her in the same way I saw a cartoon squire deliver a special gift to his lady-in-waiting.

The next day, while waiting in the handball line at first recess, Jamie came over to me and told me to come with her to the drinking fountain.

"Andrea doesn't like you anymore."

"Okay?" I answered, lilting my voice to make it almost a question.

And that was that for #6. It took a long time to get over that. I couldn't perform. I couldn't be witty or charming. I stared like a dumb ox and brought her a can of Diet Coke on a cheap metal floral tray. Don't underestimate the psychic damage this sort of thing can do.

5. Donna

AAAAAARGH. Cheerleader. Popular. Pretty. Jackpot! No. It was a disaster that led to the story about waking up, sweaty, on an otherwise empty leather couch dressed in felt. I remember we went to Medieval Times at least twice. She had one of those horrendous "murder mystery" parties at her house. She was into events and spectacles. I was and still remain a fan of doing nothing over something. But I told her I didn't really like parties and would kind of like to bail on the event.

She insisted that I go and that we go shopping for clothes. Ultimately, the fake jousting and ill-defined rules of a murder mystery party were part of the sacrifice I was willing to make. She was genuinely a nice girl, after all.

I was more of a thrift store than mall guy, and I think she honestly didn't understand why I would wear old clothes. She picked out a generic GAP plaid shirt for me to wear. Fine.

When I arrived at her house that evening before the party, she told me to wait at the door, because she had a surprise. She came downstairs in the same fucking shirt that we had purchased for me earlier in the day.

"Surprise!"

In my head, I said this:

> "Surprise? Yeah it is. A surprise to you that I'm leaving and we are done."
>
> Mic drop.

In reality, I said:

"Cool . . . that looks good on you. And if we got lost, people would know who to deliver the other one to."

But as you know, this is the least of the clothes-related issues with Donna. It wasn't unusual for people to wear custom outfits to prom; it was a custom that many of us wore period suits. Zoot suits, nineteenth-century financier suits . . . whatever. So she tells me that if I take care of the dinner plans, she'll take care of the rental prom clothes.

I went to her house a few days before prom to make sure everything fit. She brought what she had rented downstairs. It was a lot of black. It looked like a . . . holy shit! It was a bag of felt. And it was essentially one garment, a kind of tunic-meets-poncho black coverall. It also had gold trimming, black leggings, and a kind of synthetic leather knee-high boot that even a prostitute might feel was a bit tacky.[2] She wanted me to go as some kind of King Arthur to match her (slightly better, but still ridiculous) damsel in distress/dinner theatre Guinevere.

There are pictures of this. Check the back of the book. My wife has kept them because she, properly, thinks this is a combination of hilarious and pathetic. The look on my face resembles what I imagine my face would look like if you told me a monkey had just torn the jugular vein out of a mentally challenged kid and left him to bleed out. Was I horrified? Shocked? Wondering why the hell you just told me this terrible story? I think my expression is what you would find on someone's face the second before they reacted. Caught in a second of denial, contemplation, and a macabre zombie stare. However, she looks good. She was pretty hot.

---

[2] The editor asked, here in the final edit, if I should be using "sex worker" instead of prostitute. Maybe I should be. I've never thought about it. Initially I just wrote "whore" and left it at that. In the meantime, I should thank the wonderful editing team that has worked on this. Samantha Martin, Megan Bailey, and Steve Ushioda are superrad and superhelpful. Steve Byrnes, I should point out, has been the poor soul who has put up with me messing with a half dozen or more deadlines, taking a few years off his life as he looked to explain to his bosses where the hell my manuscript was.

CHAPTER 8

Call Me Maybe

Or, To All the Girls I've Broken Up with by Not Calling or Answering the Phone

A Soundtrack for Reading

1. Call Me Maybe—Carly Rae Jepsen
2. If I Could Talk I'd Tell You—The Lemon Heads
3. I've Got a Flair—Fountains of Wayne
4. Never Say Never—That Dog
5. Need You Around—Smoking Popes
6. Selfless, Cold, and Composed—Ben Folds Five
7. Calling and Not Calling My Ex—Okkervil River
8. We Rule the School—Belle and Sebastian
9. Why Bother?—Weezer
10. Please, Please, Please Let Me Get What I Want—The Smiths
11. Glycerine—Bush[1]
12. Crash—Dave Matthews Band

---

[1] The last two songs on this list are not there because I like them; rather, they are there because of their relationship to two girls on the list.

*Take me out tonight, where there's music and there's
people and they're young and alive. Driving in your
car, I never never want to go home, because I haven't
got one anymore. And, if a double-decker bus crashes
into us, to die by your side is such a heavenly way to
die. And, if a ten-ton truck kills the both of us, to die
by your side, Well, the pleasure—the privilege is mine.*

—The Smiths, "There Is a Light
That Never Goes Out"

4. Anne Watson

Anne is her real name. She is totally cool with me using it. This makes
her the coolest on the list. Easy. She is also one of my and my wife's
dearest friends to this day. So everything turned out OK. But first I
had to tell her to go fuck herself when she wouldn't allow me to win a
board game, using an answer that was technically more correct than
the answer on the back of the card.[2]

My relationship with Anne has spanned as long as any relationship that I have: twenty-three years.[3] We met when I was fourteen. I
consider her one of my closest friends. We dated for a while, though
I don't think we ever officially used the word around each other. We
never kissed. I didn't quite understand the "lean in" dynamics at the
end of a night and became so self-aware of it that the mere idea of
kissing spooked me so much that I got the jitters at the end of every
evening.

The debated question of whether we dated or not was put to
rest two decades after the supposed relationship. Anne came on the
podcast to talk about her life as a public relations director, habitual
car napper, chef, wedding planner, and photographer. My cohost Jeff
became the arbiter of a question that had dogged Anne and me for
some time. Did we ever actually date? I thought we did. She wasn't
so sure, though she recalled that we held hands in my friend Brent's
VW van, while he was driving down PCH. I don't remember that.

---

[2] AW: Sounds perfectly normal and reasonable to me.

[3] AW: Holy shit we're old!

Obviously my hands leave quite the impression.[4] Our relationship
was straight out of *Lucas*, Corey Haim's third best movie, wherein
Haim's character won't let the girl he likes see where he lives.[5] Anne
would routinely pick me up at a designated spot near the mini mart,
near where I lived. Anne and I hung out a lot and became emotionally attached.[6] She asked me to go with her to her prom. Before the
dance, however, Anne sat me down on the steps of the church and
gently dumped me. I do not remember this. She does. She remembers dumping me! You can't dump someone you've never dated!
So that must mean that we had at least been in a relationship. Jeff
agreed. I win.

Our relationship was, and still is, largely based on shared experiences and a platonic affection. But it is also crucial that we both
liked to make people laugh and were decent at it. We didn't have a
competition with each other, but egged each other on toward absurdity in taking everything one step over the line.[7]

---

[4] AW: Ha ha ha—FINE. Yes, you win. But I was thinking about this again recently . . .
Since I "broke up" with Kelly Morgan, does that mean I dated her too??? 'Cause I never
kissed her! But I had to give her the "it's not you, it's me" speech when she got too creepy . . .
I'm just sayin', I think this might still be up for debate. That, or my mother's fears of me
being a lesbian when I was in high school perhaps were founded after all?! Ha ha ha ha . . .
Hmmm. OK, fair enough. Just changed my mind—I never WANTED to kiss her. And I
guess at the time I did want to kiss you—I was just too goofy and freaked out to know what
to do and wasn't sure if you even "liked me like that." So, fine. You win. Dammit. I hate
losing. Argh.

[5] AW: what were the first two best?
  DvV: See below.
  2. *Dream a Little Dream* 1. *The Goonies*.

[6] AW: YES. Now that is the best way I could possibly put it—love that phrasing—"we
became emotionally attached." That's exactly it! I think that in my own way I was already
showing classic "codependent" personality traits that I'm still working on to this day . . . I've
learned this about myself this year. So, yes—we attached—I saw something in you that was
broken. I just felt it. And I liked feeling needed by you. It felt good to make you feel good.
We made each other laugh—feel less shitty—and I seriously think that's why we are still
friends, because somewhere, way back when, we connected on a deeper level. And that's
pretty darn cool.

[7] AW: Yes! See? I hadn't read this before I typed my previous note. That's exactly it. I think
it's a rare thing this day and age too, to actually connect on any real level with people—social
media has ruined that kind of platonic affection that can only develop when you spend time
with someone, in person. It's how you become "emotionally attached!" Makes total sense
to me!!

For instance, we found a mannequin head, and I put it on through my shirt and pulled my shirt up over my own head. We named this character Connie, and she would come out when we were bored and we would walk into stores and ask for things. It might not sound funny to you. It was damn hilarious to us. We went through the Del Taco drive-thru, with Anne hiding and moving the pedals and wheel while I demanded more "del Scorcho" sauce, as the voice of a bald mannequin. When the mannequin head prank got old, we would throw down even more mannequin fun by having "Connie" review movies or talk about important books neither of us had read. Good times. [Here I added a story about something harmless, at least I think so, but Anne has asked me not to say what it was.] During my senior year in high school, despite the tenuous friendship, we found comfort in absurdity in each other. My senior photos for the yearbook were lousy. So we took a sombrero from a local Mexican restaurant, drew a long mustache on my face, tied a red bandana around my neck, and took *señor* photos. This was admittedly racially insensitive, but without malice. Anne took some good pictures that night, but the yearbook would not publish them. At least it made us laugh. Today, Anne is a professional photographer.

Anne can tell her own stories, but the most telling about my state of mind with her and with my uncomfortable place in the world at the cusp of turning eighteen came during a game of Trivial Pursuit.

We were playing the game to a Dwight Yoakum album, from which I can only remember "The Streets of Bakersfield." This was making me unusually angry and strangely uncomfortable. It became my team's turn to answer a question for a piece of the pie, the question was, "Who were the Huguenots?" I offered an uncommonly precise answer: "French Calvinists." The answer on the card simply read: "Protestants." I explained that while "Protestants" is indeed correct, I gave a much more detailed answer, since the Huguenots were Protestants of the French Calvinist variety. Many of their pastors had been trained under Calvin himself, while exiles in Geneva. A small discussion debate turned into a heated fight.

Recounting what happened today is as exasperating as old men talking about a classic boxing match that was never televised. Imagine two old men talk about watching Joe Louis on an undercard. It was the most epic fight ever! Louis knocked the bum out in the first round! No, it went the full fifteen, and Louis won on the cards! And on and on. Everyone who was there has slightly different versions of who threw what shots and what kind of damage they did. But everyone remembers the haymaker. I landed my haymaker with the wholly inappropriate and satisfying last words: "Go fuck yourself." I left the game, got in my Volkswagen beetle, and drove off, simultaneously angry and strangely satisfied.

Part of what had made me so angry was that damn Dwight Yoakum album. Anne had been on a trip back east to visit her cousin, and she came back listening to Shania Twain.[8] This baffled us all, but me especially, since the two of us were indie savants. We could talk about the distinctions between post-punk and college rock. We disliked the Smithereens and the Replacements but appreciated the earnest yelps of the Catherine Wheel and This Mortal Coil as well as the disaffected slackers in Pavement. Our mixtapes were epic. And now this?

Therefore, the fact that Dwight Yoakum was playing on the stereo is important. Kyle made a point of playing the music with no irony intended. Anne, who had recently apostatized from the church of Sub Pop and Matador, was praising the choice of contemporary middle-of-the-road country music. I felt abandoned by my friends who seemed completely fine with all this. What? No jokes? No dissecting the lyrics about small-town America? C'mon! He had to have written that song precisely for Gillette or Budweiser to pick up and use for a commercial. No one sees this? No one?

They probably did. But Anne was the mature one among our friends. She rose above the petty, ironic disses of certain musical styles. She was less jaded. She didn't need an extra shield or distance from the world, because she was adjusted. Sure, she still dug the Pixies, but she also found adult contemporary country pop appealing. She wasn't afraid to be "caught" listening to music; she played whatever the hell she wanted. I, however, wasn't ready to pull back the layer of ironic insulation I needed to shield myself from the world. She had also signaled to the rest of my friends that they might also shed some of the protective layers that *they* didn't need. She

---

[8] AW: Does it help that I fucking HATE her music now? So, I understand the anger it made you feel. And for that, I sincerely apologize. Too late?

became a kind of ringleader of our friends, one that I was extremely jealous of for being funnier and more lighthearted and less emotionally draining than I knew I was.[9] And so, telling her to fuck herself felt good.[10] She was ruining whatever value my ironic posturing was worth. And without that, I was just a depressed kid trying to find friends, acceptance, and real human interaction. She would not ruin me. I would land the haymaker.

We didn't hang out for some time.

We talked the summer before she left for college. Everything was cool. Anne went to college in Washington. I went to visit her when her parents bought me tickets in exchange for babysitting Anne's twin brothers. They were in junior high, so they really didn't need watching.

I flew to Seattle to see a friend with whom a friendship had been restored. So, of course, I figured a romantic relationship would naturally develop. She hated her university, so I was a welcome diversion. She had recently pledged a sorority. That was shocking enough. But it also meant that she would not be available much during the week I was there. I spent much of the time wandering the streets of Seattle with my Walkman. I remember that it was especially rainy and I had the cassette "Camels, Spilled Coronas and Mariachi Bands" by J Church. When I play the album, I can still feel the rain and the depression. On one of the evenings, Anne invited me to a sorority party to carve pumpkins. I still have no idea what sororities do. But this one, at least, liked to carve pumpkins and let a senior in high school join in the festivities. They were friendly and laughed at my various pumpkin jokes. At one point, the knife slipped and cut my wrist right across the artery. As blood began to spurt out, I'm sure either Anne or I was quick enough to make a *Carrie* joke. Later in life, when I would see a psychologist or go to the doctor, I was always self-conscious about being depressed and suicidal and having a scar across my left wrist. "It was a pumpkin carving accident, I swear!"

---

[9] AW: Naw, Dan—seriously? Did you feel that way? I never saw myself as a "ringleader"— how weird. It's funny how other people perceive us vs. how we perceive ourselves, isn't it?

[10] AW: Is it nuts that I just smiled when I read that, because—see?! I like making you feel good! Even at my own expense! Ha ha . . . hello codependent personality disorder!

My time in Washington ended, and I flew back home (my first flight ever) and was served a vodka tonic on the plane. It felt good. It reminded me of stealing vodka from the cupboard or drinking it with my friends from the apartment complex. I came back, aware of the allure of alcohol. It scared me enough that I swore off alcohol altogether. In fact, I never had a drink during my senior year in high school, at least until the last day of school. If anything else was around, I justified myself in doing drugs that weren't mine. You aren't really doing drugs if they aren't yours. This is addict logic.

Stay with this story. Here it takes a turn for the worse. And it may be one of the worst things I've ever done.

Anne transferred to a school in California. For my birthday, she planned out a strangely cathartic birthday present. We drove around to every house where I'd lived, from the mountains, to Riverside, and then back to Irvine. It was well planned and tame enough. But it had just enough possible suspiciousness that I didn't tell April (#2 on the list), who I was dating at the time.

During our road adventure, Anne and I were in a mountain village when she asked me why we weren't dating. Seriously. Anne asked this. I promise! My response? "Sure, I'm dating April right now, as you know, but that won't last too long. Why don't we start dating when my relationship with April ends."

Seriously.

Let this sink in.[11]

I told a girl that I'd like to date her but *after* I finished my relationship with someone else. And this wasn't like "I'll go dump *x* so we can be together." It was, "Huh. Cool. Well, I'm digging this one

---

[11] AW: I did. A lot. And ya know what? I remember now that I cried when I got home that night. Mostly because I seem to recall helping you in some way to buy something for April or help you do something romantic for her . . . I don't remember exactly. I just remember feeling like the biggest shithead with so little self-respect that I LET you say that to me, after planning that whole day and driving you around and reminiscing about your childhood with you, etc. And then not only did I let you say that to me, but I pretended it rolled off my shoulders and then HELPED you "romance" the girl who you were "currently dating." This is why I had so few boyfriends. Zero self-respect, seriously. What was wrong with me?! I should have clocked you upside the head! But I'm glad I didn't—because it all worked out as it was supposed to—life always does. And I'm sure glad I get to still be friends with you and Beth Anne twenty-three years later!

girl now, but you know, things don't last, so if you wait your turn in line."

What an asshole.[12]

There are other stories like this. But that's the one you need to know to get the point. I was a self-conscious and awkward kid, jacked up on adolescent hormones and just enough charm to cause some damage.

3. Melissa Lu

I think we started dating around my birthday. Or her birthday. Or maybe our birthdays are close together. There was a party, and it came on the heels of some high school theatre production we were both in. The party was at her house, and I remember following her around, trying to get into a conversation. With many of my girl-friends, I can pinpoint exact times, locations, historical timestamps, and so on, but not with Melissa. Melissa was more of a season than a discreet amount of time. We might have dated for four weeks or four months. For whatever reason, she is one girl with whom I have no clear recollection of the actual time when we were together. My mind had been getting more and more erratic around this time, and I wasn't yet on prescribed medication.

I don't remember when we started dating, and I can't remember exactly how we broke up. I remember some of the surrounding circumstances but few of the precise details.

I probably decided to ask her out when someone told someone that she might say yes. I can't remember our first date, but it was probably at the damn Golden Spoon. We didn't really have coffee shops then, so we would meet at local places, and in the mid '90s—I cannot stress this enough—froyo was fucking huge. I was infatuated with Melissa. She was . . . exotic. Which isn't to point out that she was Asian, which she was (and is).[13] She was pretty in an unconventional way and cool in a self-deprecating, offbeat way. This

---

[12] AW: Yep. But you're one of my favorite assholes in the whole world! Ha ha!

[13] ML: And continues to be.

sounds terrible. As if I'm objectifying her as her ethnic origin.[14] And this was pre-*Pinkerton* Weezer, so I wasn't just aping Rivers Cuomo. She was legitimately pretty in a kind of grown-up, runway-model kind of way (she later went on to be a successful pop star in Asia).[15] She was the first girl I had a regular "kissing relationship" with, which probably sounds lame.[16] And was, but I was really so infatuated and terrified with the idea of a girlfriend up to this point that I had tended to keep most girlfriends at an awkward distance, just in case I had to bolt.

Earlier, if I had tried to find girls who would fix me, girls who I thought were stable, Melissa seemed like someone on whom I was taking a flyer. She was not going to "fix" me. She was in a similar social bracket to mine: well-known at school but unconventional, maybe mysteriously popular. I remember driving with her up to LA to get modeling pictures taken and thinking that I was dating someone who would certainly end up famous. She gave me some of the proofs from her modeling shoot, and I kept them in my wallet to impress people I knew from other schools.[17]

She had parents that I saw as the opposite of mine, albeit suboptimal in their own way. Her parents fit the stereotype of overbearing Asian parents that would rather have their children's fingers bleed from violin practice than crack an occasional smile. This is a terrible stereotype, I'm sure her parents are great people, but the vibe they threw at me was real.[18] Melissa and I started dating when . . . well, I don't remember anything about it. I was seventeen, and this was the year of whirlwind relationships and the realization that there was something wrong with me. In earlier recollections of this relationship, Melissa was a kind of footnote, an afterthought to my tempestuous seventeenth year. But the more I thought about circumstances relating to my desperate need to love and to be loved (or like and be

---

[14] ML: So I probably should be pretty pissed or offended or something with this, but then again, Dan was the whitest guy I'd ever met. So this categorization makes sense.

[15] ML: Successful is a definite overstatement. One-hit wonder is more apropos, but I appreciate the props.

[16] ML: Hey! Samesies!

[17] ML: I sincerely hope those have died in a fire.

[18] ML: Def real. They were not down with you. Nor anyone else that I dated. But now I get it. 'Cause I'm a mom now. And I will kill anyone who comes close to my son. #tigermom

liked?),[19] we spent a remarkable amount of time together. I remember seeing Bush, No Doubt, and the Suicide Machines play at the Pond/Honda Center in Anaheim.[20] We definitely made out to my cassette single of Bush's "Glycerine," which was the B-side on the cassette single to "Machine Head."[21] "Glycerine" was "our song," which wasn't the worst song, and I had to spend a few years pretending to be embarrassed by it. Although it is certainly better than "More than Words" by Extreme, which was my song with Carly Jansen during the summer before high school.[22]

Melissa was a great gal, but the relationship didn't have a fair shot at success. You see, throughout this time, mental illness began to manifest itself with my first suicidal thoughts.[23] So I began to distance myself from Melissa. I began to isolate and occasionally see old friends who had new substances, and I eventually fell in with a group of kids who spent their weekends at all-age ska shows (this was Third Wave Ska and Orange County was its epicenter, with bands like No Doubt and Sublime setting the tone early and lesser known but beloved bands like Reel Big Fish, My Superhero, and Save Ferris).[24] The golden rule of this scene was to not "sell out." That is, we didn't want the bands we liked to actually make money, nor did we want them to get popular enough that anyone else would listen to them. I had been dabbling in this scene for a while, but when I jumped in, I knew Melissa had to be on the way out. I figured she couldn't hang with a scene like this.[25] I knew this because she bought a Reel Big Fish shirt.

---

[19] ML: In retrospect, this desperate need to be liked totally makes sense and was in line with your behavior.

[20] ML: That was fun!
    DvV: I didn't really like it.

[21] ML: So many awesome things about that sentence.

[22] DvV: It is worth noting, the first song that I could really dig as an "our song" was "Our Way to Fall" by Yo La Tengo with my wife, which we would have danced to at our wedding, if her parents allowed dancing. Also, I should note that "Arthur's Theme" by Christopher Cross or something by Air Supply might be "our song" with Beth Anne, because . . . well, karaoke.

[23] ML: Holy shit.

[24] ML: You introduced me to ska that, true story, actually inspired a song I ended up writing for an album. For that, I thank you, I think.

[25] ML: You were probably right.

The shirt embarrassed me to no end. First of all, I was sure that she didn't really like them. She only went to one show but came back wearing the shirt. She didn't have the cred to wear it. She was invading my scene. And because people knew that it was *my* scene, her identifying with it tied the two of us back together in other people's heads. I thought people would start to think that maybe *I too lacked cred*. Second, she went to those shows to track me down (which she admitted). So I figured that it was inappropriate to wear a shirt from a tracking expedition. Third, the whole scene was going to shit anyway, and most of us knew it. When she wore the shirt, we interpreted it as an omen that the scene was preparing to jump the shark. But ultimately, it embarrassed me because I was a colossal asshole.[26]

One of her last ditch efforts to be kind toward me coincided with one of my first fits of neurotic rage and uncontrollable shaking.[27] Her strategy involved an elaborate scavenger hunt that ended on a fake island in the middle of a fake lake. It was sweet, but I was in no mood.[28] I was to go to my car after a rehearsal for some theater event and then, based on the clue I received, drive to another location to pick up another clue, and so on, and so on, until I finally found her with a lovely picnic on the fake island in the middle of town. After about three clues, low on gas and frustrated with my dumb 1988 Colt Vista, I pulled into a center that had a shop that made those giant novelty cookies (giant novelty cookies have played a disproportionately prominent role in complicated relationships, throughout my life). I remember crawling into my back seat and starting to bite my arm and muffle a scream. My feet and hands started to shake. I remember thinking that I was legitimately losing the plot. I had images of white jackets and padded rooms and figured it was just a matter of time before I was sent off to an institution. I felt frustrated and angry and couldn't shake it. It was more than just frustration and anger. These were emotions I had learned to swallow or punch out.[29]

---

[26] ML: True story—you were a colossal asshole toward the end of our relationship. Granted, I probably had braces and was all gangly, so I can only blame you so much for that.

[27] ML: Holy shit again.

[28] ML: Elaborate scavenger hunts only arise from last-ditch efforts to continue high school relationships.

[29] ML: Holy shit × 3. I legitimately had no idea this was going on, and I don't know if I would have believed it even if you had told me.

This was despair, and yet for no real reason. It had nothing to do with Melissa at all. And if anything, I thought that girlfriends were supposed to cure this by serving as evidence of normalcy, by having them validate me to a larger group of people, and sometimes, just by being nice to me when things were shitty.

Huddled in the backseat of my car, and out of view, I scribbled down a few notes on a piece of paper. I needed to mark this strange moment of despair and actually write out: I am going to kill myself.[30] That kind of worked. Whoa! All I had to do was promise myself a way out at some point, and I could get a grip, at least for the moment.

I ended up lying there for some time only to arrive late at the fake island. I muttered something to Melissa about being cold, and we were soon on our way. There was a giant novelty cookie that I took and kept in my car to sustain me for the next day or so. I don't know whether she brought it, it was part of the scavenger hunt, or I had purchased it during my mental breakdown.

A floodgate had opened, though. And I had no healthy outlet for what got released. I had freaked myself out and couldn't tell anyone. Certainly not Melissa. So somehow the relationship came to an end. I'm betting it involved me getting anxious and distant and ignoring calls or pages or however the hell we communicated in 1996.[31]

After we broke up, she showed up at a CD release party for the Reel Big Fish album that spawned their first radio single and video. The show had sold out, and I figured that her being there was proof that she was either lame for now liking bands that I liked and/or she was "stalking" me.[32]

This makes absolutely no sense, so I am certain it is what I actually thought.

Don't ask why *I* was there if it was such a sell-out thing to do. Perhaps I should have abandoned the Galaxy Theatre that night and gone to see some crappy band playing in the converted skating rink in Huntington Beach. Nevertheless, that autumn, my love affair with the local ska scene died. Melissa was gone, though our paths would keep crossing throughout our senior year. I moved on to date

---

[30] ML: Jeezus. I am so sorry that you were going through this. Seriously.

[31] ML: That all sounds about right.

[32] ML: You dick. Although you were probably correct.

a cheerleader, the one that had me wear the felt costume and plastic boots to prom. I moved from third-wave ska back to 4AD bands, and an obsession with moody Brit pop. If I was going to be mopey, I didn't need all that happy, horn-infused ska nonsense. I was growing into Morrissey. I'm not going to blame him and the Smiths for my first dive into a serious depression, but they didn't help.[33]

2. April Anderson

April Anderson was a junior during my senior year of high school. She had met me in a theatre class and had seen me run through girl-friends the way a choosy shopper looks through the racks for the right shirt. If my earlier relationships had been disasters because of my severe lack of self-esteem, this one would suffer from impulses on the opposite end of the spectrum: an overwhelming, though fraudulent, appearance of self-confidence. By this time, I had left the old gang at my first high school, and made the covert transfer to the school

---

[33] ML: Now that I know that Dan had a substance abuse problem, I feel like I can attribute a lot of his behavior to that. So, Dan remembered a lot of stuff that I didn't remember, although there were definitely a lot of details that he got spot on. Like, how he was a complete dick during my fake island scavenger hunt, which yes, was a last-ditch effort to maintain our weird relationship. My thoughts on our fleeting high school relationship (before I knew about his substance abuse problem): He had transferred from another school, which made him cool. I think he was also one of the few kids in HS that had dabbled in "real" entertainment (i.e. he had an agent and/or went on commercial auditions), which made him super cool to us "drama kids." We definitely shared an offbeat, self-deprecating sense of humor that Dan mentioned, so that was certainly attractive. And also, he seemed like a nice guy.

Here's the thing: as we started dating, he started gaining popularity with non-drama groups in high school. And although I was kinda popular in other groups, well, it was high school, so insecurity runs rampant in most every kid, including me and definitely Dan. I think I thought that he was becoming more popular and leaving me behind.

But, in retrospect and now knowing about his issues, I can see that Dan wasn't just an insecure transfer student. There easily could have been a darker side that even if I had known about it, I don't think I would have believed it. He had a palpable and desperate need to be liked. He was always kind of jittery, nervous, and a little on edge. At first, I thought it was charming; in retrospect, I can see it was now symptomatic. He never chatted much about his own family, and he suffered terrible mood swings. Superficially, I could see how he passed himself off as a normal, functioning adolescent, but jeezus, that is some baggage to be carrying around at age seventeen. Very happy to see all of the success that has come to him in his adult life.

across town. I already recounted the basic facts, but the way in which I transferred is worth mentioning.

Today, if you want to transfer schools (especially to the school to which I did), you have to go on a waiting list and then have your parents provide certifications from birth to immunization to three types of residency verification. They even threaten parents with up to four years in prison for lying about their student's address. You can't even pull an Andrea Zuckerman/Gabrielle Carteris and use your grandma's address and then bus into West Beverly High. But in 1995, you could have your friend Brent drive you over to the school office a few weeks before school started, ask for a transfer sheet, go outside, forge a signature, and turn it back in. *Voila!*

If I count the twenty-three girls with whom I had some kind of relationship, between ages eleven to twenty, the one that's most difficult to write and think about was my ten-month relationship with April Anderson. It was a heartfelt, cliché, disastrous, and wonderful high school romance. Mentioning her name around different friends from high school evoked responses like, "Yeah? You dated *her*?" This usually was accompanied by raised eyebrows and a nod of approval or squinting eyes and a bemused smile as if to ask, "You dated the cheerleader? Was that for real or just superironic?"[34] It was a kind of social win on my part with both groups, but it wasn't ironic at all. I believed there was some kind of real human connection.

During my junior year, I hardly knew her. April was like a minor league player you keep hearing about but hasn't made it to the bigs yet. You've heard good things, but it might be a while before you see them in action. This created a certain level of intrigue but not enough to keep one's attention for too long. Maybe it was because her name had the alliteration of two strong *A*'s. Maybe it was because it was a name that sounded like it belonged on a teenage drama set somewhere near the coast, or maybe I'm reading back everything into the name having experienced hearing it and saying it so often during a formative time in my life.

Certain relationships involve a wicked cocktail of hormones, social pressure, pop songs, and spare time. This can hurl two people together for an awkward, rushed, panicked yet sublime period before

---

[34] AA: It was more of the latter . . . you were WAY cooler than I was, let's be honest.

they crash and burn, leaving a scar that never really goes away. But, unlike a battle scar, it eventually recedes from your memory, and you eventually just accept as part of you and who you became.

There never was a real chance that April and I would still be in a relationship ten years later. Hell, the chances of having a relationship longer than a *month* were slim. I was the coolly detached kid in thrift-store clothes, with a connection to MTV and an aloof detachment that looked like elitism to some, but in reality was borne from crippling anxiety.

April was involved with everything. Her mom was a beloved teacher at the school. She was outgoing without being obnoxious and always laughing without seeming like a sycophant when laughing at others' jokes.[35] Mixing an adjusted, pretty girl from a good family in a peculiar part of the world with a kid who wanted to belong but couldn't for various reasons was dangerous. Add her cheerleading, friends across the social spectrum, and large breasts, and I should have seen that this was a doomed relationship. I don't bring up that last point to sexualize her, but rather, because the growth of breasts has to be the most bewildering and socially awkward issue among teenage girls.[36] Guys have no equivalent. If I were to whittle down every problem between guys and girls between the ages of twelve and eighteen, 75 percent of them would involve, in some form or another, breasts.[37]

She knew me as the slightly older, confident, and popular guy. We had a theatre class together; she and I were paired up to do an improv scene. Having been a professional improv comedian (discussed in a later chapter), I was regularly called upon to spend the entire period on stage doing improvisational scenes with other students. This was the first time anyone at any school had seen me perform in my element. It took a lot of practice, but it was an actual tangible skill that I once had.[38] From a few times being on stage with her and with a few mutual friends from theatre and the rare party I

---

[35] AA: This is so sweet!

[36] AA: Amen!

[37] AA: HAHAHAHA! Lol.

[38] AA: You were so good, Dan, the drama teacher, Mr. Trevino, literally left you on stage sweating under the lights the entire period for his own amusement. You were SO funny!

would attend after football games, we became friendly. I think she was insecure as a sophomore,[39] but this is my composite picture of a character I once knew, but only from a foggy high school, hormonal, fearful, and anxiety-induced point of view.[40]

She was a rare hybrid—both dancer and cheerleader—which was like being a vegan and a deer hunter: you couldn't win with either crowd while being with both. I suspected a certain level of interest when she and a friend wrote on my car window with Dijon mustard a few times.[41]

This behavior counted as flirting sometime during the last century. They referred to me as "Cliff." I had once named various people as "Cliff," as in, they were such inconsequential people, if they walked off of a cliff you wouldn't notice.[42] It's a horrid concept, but at least wittier than the more recent analog: "Bye Felicia."

I talked like this, because I was . . . again . . . an asshole.

They also referenced being a "lurker." This was some name for people that hung around the parking lot during breaks and stood adjacent to groups conversing. These people were trying to fit in, but not being able to, just "lurked" around one group to the next. Of course, these two ideas came easily to me, as I was terrified of being found out as a fraud, a cliff, and a lurker.

After realizing she had some kind of interest, enough to vandalize my car with mustard, I figured she might be the next girlfriend as my then current relationship was winding down and I was planning on jumping ship.[43] Seriously. This is what I did. If I didn't know that it came from a place of crippling insecurity and fear, I would nominate myself as the *biggest* asshole I'd ever met. Insecurity or not, however, this was a pretty disgraceful way of acting. I escaped the last girlfriend and decided to start hanging around April. It started sometime after Halloween 1996.

---

[39] AA: YES.

[40] AA: Spot on.

[41] AA: OMG me and [name redacted]! We both had a crush on you . . . I completely forgot about this embarrassing demonstration of affection!

[42] AA: HAHAHA, oh wow, I'm dying. How do you remember all this?!

[43] AA: So stupid, I'm sorry about that . . . The poor Vista!

There was a party at someone's clubhouse: these were communal places for people who lived in apartments, albeit rich people apartments. In my hometown, roughly 85 percent of all underage drinking took place at these clubhouses.[44] It was a big enough party, and I had just pulled off the con job of social status jumping, so that I could arrive with confidence and try to pull off an ironic and clever costume. I decided that I could throw on a hoody, aviator glasses and draw a mustache. I would go as the composite sketch of the Unabomber. I rarely nail Halloween costumes—I've worn maybe four in my life—but I was proud of this one. I earned just the right amount of ironic chuckles, bemused looks, and bewilderment from those who weren't following the news.

I don't know what anyone else wore. Except April. She dressed as Catwoman. She later rued this fact.[45] I stayed late at the party, which ironically involved no drinking. After chatting with one of April's friends I eventually made it to over to the table where April was sitting. The Catwoman costume was significant not because it was sexy (though it was). Rather, I was impressed that she went all in when others (like me, admittedly) tried to do just enough to not be shamed for *not* wearing something. Granted, the shiny black faux latex made it easy for me to find her. I awkwardly tried to strike up a conversation. Not too difficult, right? After all, we had been casual acquaintances, and she had written messages to me with condiments. I don't actually remember talking to her. I only remember the seemingly shy girl who wasn't afraid to go all in with a costume without a trace of irony. It was refreshing.[46]

Around midnight, someone made a comment about feeling bad for those who had to take the SAT the next morning. The November 1 SAT was the last one you could take to meet most university's deadlines.

Shit.

---

[44] AA: Haha, yep.

[45] AA: I still shudder to think about it . . . bleh.

[46] AA: I was so happy you were talking to me. I stayed quiet because I didn't want to offend you or say something stupid. You always filled the silence, so I just figured I could sit still in silence, smile, and look interested in everything you had to say. I fixated on your smile; I loved your smile!

I forgot I signed up to do that. I should have remembered the effect on Zack and Jessie getting into Yale and Stansbury (the Harvard of the West) and the stress it caused. Kids at my school spent thousands of dollars to prepare for this seminal moment. I went in to the testing room with small desks and took the test the next morning, rushing through sections and falling asleep before the timer went off. I hadn't really given college a thought, and thus had not studied for these strange examinations, which, now as a college professor, I can assure you don't tell you that much about a student's quality.

I wasn't stressed because I had little interest in college. Such a sentiment was unthinkable at my high school: *everyone* went to college. The fact that I wasn't sure if I wanted to go never came up in conversation. I had assumed a middling GPA would land me somewhere, maybe for a brief stint. *I* would act or write, and the rest of those chumps could spend four more years in an academic prison. Have at it, guys.

I scored remarkably well, given my antipathy: 1490. This was just shy of Zack Morris's fictional (and technically impossible) 1502.[47] People started asking me what college I would go to. Before I had this score attached to my record, I assumed I would never go to college. This was pre-Internet, so I must have looked at some brochure at school and seen that Emerson College was good if you wanted to go into broadcasting. I decided I would go there. I had no idea how that worked. I never filled out the application. I learned the deadline to Emerson had passed, but our California state schools would let you apply later in the year, so I copied my friend Kyle's routine and applied to all the UC schools. He got into UCLA. I was rejected by all eleven. No one told me I had to pass Algebra 2 to get into a UC. I have still never passed Algebra 2. All of this would affect the fate of my relationship with April Anderson.[48]

---

[47] AA: I was waiting to read a *Saved by the Bell* reference from you.

[48] AA: OK, stop. I truly do not believe that you were this "dim" on the subject of college. Everyone around you was filling out applications, talking about it, ramping up for it . . . Dan, you were so smart, and yet, you always sabotaged yourself. I thought it was because you wanted people to feel badly for you . . . you enjoyed being "the kid from the other side of the tracks," crazy family, blah, blah, blah . . . you made sure we always remembered that label . . . You did it to yourself, and why, I'll never understand. Well, actually, maybe I will after I read

This would be a relationship of a completely different magnitude. It would be more physical and emotional than I had bargained for. I had gone from girlfriends out of Beach Boys songs into a relationship from a gritty cable drama. This was like going from cigarettes to cocaine in terms of intensity. Ironically, in fact, I went from the latter to the former during this time. I may not have known then that this would be a different relationship, but I was willing on some level to attempt some kind of real human connection with someone. I don't know if it was initially a determination that I had to date her for some social status, or physical attraction, or a sense that she might be more than just a lily pad from which I was jumping from each to each seeking some kind of self-confidence. But it started, and for ten months, it ran the gamut of emotions. It also started to reveal some of the deep cracks I had been trying to hide since grade school.

It was mid-November 1996. For some reason, I was on campus late one evening. I saw her near the Coke machines. She didn't have a car, so I offered her a ride in my newly acquired 1972 green VW Beetle. In a sea of cars bought by wealthy parents, my Beetle stood out as a sign of class defiance (or so I thought). I covered it with stickers of bands like That Dog and Pavement and Yo La Tengo. I built my own speaker system with pieces of leftover home stereos. I spent whatever money I had trying to upgrade everything I could.[49]

I offered April a ride home, and when we got to her house, I did what I was rarely ever capable of doing. I jumped in with both feet. I leaned in to kiss her, and she reciprocated. This was like an agoraphobic running through a crowded mall or a scared cat scampering through a rainstorm on wet concrete. Before I learned how to make real decisions as an adult, I would sometimes find myself with a brief moment of courage to do something sudden and terrifying. It's how I decided I would get married and go to grad school. Too scared to think twice, I thought once and went against my own judgment. We kissed. She said good-bye and got out of the car, and I felt a euphoria akin to later substance-fueled highs, and the peak drunken glee in

---

this book . . . you were, and probably still are, one of the most talented and smart people I know. I wanted you to pick yourself up, dust yourself off, and move on.

[49] AA: I can still smell that mix of gasoline, oil, and seat upholstery when I close my eyes . . . it was a drafty car too. I was always cold riding in it.

which one basks before passing out. This romance stimulated a pleasure center in my brain, but it wasn't just physical; it was some kind of surreal life moment. I drove immediately to a friend's house and told him what I did. He was kind enough to mirror my excitement. I was like a thirteen-year-old girl who was just patted on the head by Nick Lachey—1997 Nick Lachey that is, since Nick might get a visit from the cops for doing that three decades later.[50]

I sought her out the next day at school. Actually, I kind of just lurked around her, but she gave me a subtle smile of recognition that let me know everything was cool. We were a genuinely happy high school couple, albeit immature and clueless. We had passes to Disneyland. I went to football games to see her cheer. She came to whatever school event I was performing in or hosting. Despite sneers from some of my protohipster friends, all was well. About five months into the relationship, I was getting used to this being the new normal.[51] So of course, I tried to self-sabotage. I "cheated" on her once with Kathy Sorenson.[52] Kathy was another "gal Friday" friend who would talk through whatever existential crises I was having over a frozen yogurt at the Golden Spoon. Again, this froyo shit was huge in 1997; it is baffling that it was so big, as confusing as the popularity of Furbies, Anamanaguchi, and Nick Lachey. Kathy and I made out during an ASB retreat (that's short for Associated Student Body, a student leadership/government body, which comprised the most self-important kids in high school. More on the awkward retreat kiss later).[53] My involvement with ASB was a wedge between April and me. While I was dating April, she was busy cheerleading and dancing. She had limited free time, and I would spend some of it doing inconsequential things with some

---

[50] AA: Me too, me too!!! I called [name redacted, same name from earlier] right away to rub it in her face . . . ah, what a "Mean Girl" moment!

[51] AA: We had so much fun. #2651

DvV: I have no idea what #2651 is. But if we were using hashtags in 1996 we were early to the party. I'm assuming 51 is a reference to me as it was always my favorite number. So I assume she was #26?

[52] AA: ASSHOLE! j/k.

[53] AA: ASBHC.

DvV: Well played. That stood for "Associated Student Body Hard Core" because we thought adding HC to anything was especially douche-y. I think it started with an actual sticker that had HBHC, for, "Huntington Beach Hard Core."

kind of strangely school-sanctioned group of elected kids with no actual authority. However, we student body leaders were convinced we were a big fucking deal. So we had "important" meetings and retreats to discuss how to improve school spirit, promote recycling day, and decide what kind of matching polo shirts we would all buy to wear on meeting days. At one of these retreats, we all slept on the ground at someone's house, and Kathy and I slept next to each other in our respective sleeping bags. We started kissing. It started with one of those faux tickling things as an excuse to get closer.

I swear, sons, if you are reading this book before you graduate high school, you *may not* do this. Not because it's bad *per se*, but because it is a superlame way to try to kiss a girl. The kissing led to a date: we saw Howard Stern's *Private Parts*, a surprisingly touching autobiographical film and dedication of love to his wife. Too bad he ended up getting divorced several years after the movie came out. We drove home from the theatre and kissed at a stoplight, where someone saw us. I was easy to recognize in my conspicuous VW Beetle. Who was it? Rachel Hartman? Teresa Bowman? Whoever it was, it was someone in ASB with "connections." Kathy and I called it off, and I went back to my exclusive relationship with April.[54]

On my eighteenth birthday, she sent a coded message to my beeper. To understand this, you have to have lived in a very particular window between beepers as signifiers of drug dealing or medical emergencies and the rise of the first bulky cell phones. My friend Anne was in town (yes, #4 Anne) and this is where the story of Lake Arrowhead and me putting Anne on the embarrassing "waiting list" fits in. Later that night, out of guilt, I took flowers to April. I figured that some show of affection, something I was learning to cultivate for selfish gain, would make her happy and, more important, give me peace of mind.

Time—and a decade of addiction—has a way of letting you forget things. I think there is also some little grace in forgetting or being unable to recall certain past events. I can't remember any fights, except toward the end when she would drink, and I would get angry

---

[54] AA: I knew about the cheating, but I didn't want to create drama and lose you. I felt helpless and guilty that I left you alone so much for extracurricular activities. I told myself it was my fault you cheated because I made you turn to someone else. See, Dan, I was just as insecure as you!

at her being drunk. Oh, the irony. I always wonder whether I pressured her into physical affection.[55] There was something very sweet, in a profound way, to this relationship. Maybe unremarkable, but for a lonely and insecure kid, this felt like some kind of real connection. We would find empty parking lots to make out in. She had some kind of SUV-type car with tinted windows, which was more convenient than my Beetle with its awkward bucket seats. We did have one particular incident that involved sleeping over at a house where I was housesitting, fumbling with our clothes and awkwardly trying to do something that we couldn't (or didn't want) to go through with. I told her I wanted to spend the rest of my life with her (hellooooo, insecurity), and she was understandably frightened by my being so upfront.[56]

The next morning, Anne called me, out of the blue, and asked to meet me. April spent the night at the house where I was staying, and I sneaked out to meet Anne.[57] I had barely sat down with my coffee when Anne informed me that she wanted to meet in order to let me know that she never wanted to see me again. She wanted me out of her life for good.

I went back to the condo where April was getting up and ready to leave. I wrote April a note, and she reciprocated. I would pay $500 dollars to see either of these notes, since I can't recall what we wrote, but it involved one of the most terrifyingly intimate moments of my life. School was out, and while she had various cheer and dance camps to attend, I had nothing. One of her camps was at Stanford, and she brought me back a shirt, which stuck around me for a long time. Ironically, it became Beth Anne's to wear around the house, until it started to fall apart.

I was getting decent work in LA, working for MTV and shooting various print and regional ads. But then I entered what I later

---

[55] AA: I think every teenage guy does, and no teenage girl has the self-esteem to really say "no" properly.

DvV: (*Cringes, slightly nods, moves on quickly.*)

[56] AA: This TOTALLY freaked me out. I just wanted to be a senior in high school.

[57] AA: Really? I thought I left after the awkward conversation and went back to my house to sleep . . .

DvV: I remember you hanging around, and we listened to that Jewel album in the morning.

learned was one of my first massive depressive spells. I stopped thinking about anything but the fact that all my friends would be leaving. I started to deliver pizzas after the MTV gig ended, and once fall arrived, everyone went off to the colleges to which they properly applied and were accepted. I spent hours driving around listening to "Video" by Ben Folds. I remember rewinding and listening to the line:

> Well I've seen some old friends sort of die
> or just turn into what must've been inside them
> whatever all of us had then in common grew up
> and went home

I spent the fall of what should have been my first semester at junior college doing nothing. The euphoria of drink and cheap highs was long gone, and so I was left to stew in my own mind.

I was increasingly despondent, medicated neither with prescriptions nor with booze.

I clutched on to a few things—namely, music and my rapidly deteriorating relationship with April. We had made the deal to see each other at least once a week. She was still in high school, and I was entering dangerous territory as the once popular high school kid who never got over it. One night, when we had planned to do something, she told me that she had to stay at home to be with a friend who was going through some tough times. She said we could meet at the Denny's restaurant in the University Marketplace, this one not to be confused with the TMP. She said she could pay because she had a gift certificate. I think she knew the end was coming and didn't want me spending money on her.[58] I walked her to her car after a meal of cheap food and terse conversation and saw that she had a pillow and packed bag. As we talked at her car, a friend of hers drove by and told her that she would see her later at Carly's house.

Damn.

The jig was up. I was mad but didn't want to scare her with any kind of lashing out. She made up a story on the spot about going to a

---

[58] AA: Exactly—sheesh, so embarrassing . . .
     DvV: Really! I knew it!

party for a brief time to get her friend and then take her home. I spent the evening doing my characteristic thing: driving around town listening to music that depressed me. Once I realized that wasn't helping, I decided to stick a finger in the wound and drive past the house where the party was taking place. I saw her car, and then . . . she was on the front lawn with other girls. My green Beetle was conspicuous of course, so when I got home she called me, drunk and apologetic.[59] I was hurt but felt that I was a major creep for checking on her. It was all over now. We spent the next few weeks seeing each other intermittently. I didn't show up for casting calls but instead spent time visiting friends who went to local colleges. Other times, I would just sit in coffee shops with headphones on. One night, I decided I would use flowers as a token of affection again. I called her from a payphone: there was no beeper code long enough to ask to swing by on a school night for just a few minutes. She said I could come over, but briefly. I had to meet her a few doors down from her house. Her parents couldn't know we were meeting. I gave her the flowers, and she gave me what I interpreted as a kind of pitying "that's sweet" followed by, "I have something for you too; it isn't ready yet, but I'll leave it on the windshield of my car during my dance practice on Tuesday."

Two nights later, I went to her car at the dance studio and found a four-page letter. Looking back it was sappy and probably written with the panic of a hostage writing a letter to an outsider to give to the police. I knew that it was a break up letter. She quoted Dave Matthews and the song "Candle on the Water" from *Pete's Dragon*.[60]

---

[59] AA: This was so lame . . . I was at a slumber party and crying because you saw me. End of trust = end of relationship. I was so stupid for not being honest with you, but I felt you were very fragile . . . We had lost what we had that summer I think.

[60] AA: OMG CRINGE! I'm dying inside right now reading this from embarrassment . . . I didn't know how to break up with you. I couldn't watch you cry again, and I thought the phone would be worse than a letter you could read over and over again . . . so dumb. As an adult, I am so sorry about this. The "Candle on the Water" song was my way of letting you know I thought the relationship had morphed from us being supportive of each other to me being your emotional caretaker of sorts, and it was too much for me. I thought the song was sweet, a way for you to think that I would still be there (even though I was trying to run as far away as possible). No real words would have made any of it easy at the time; I'm glad we can poke fun at my stupid analogy.

DvV: We can poke fun at it. And I did for a long time to make the sting go away.

She called, of all people, Kathy Sorensen to make sure to meet me at the Golden Spoon after I got the letter. Once again, we all went to a yogurt store, all the time. This needs to be the subject of some sociological study when looking back at the '90s. Kathy, knowing the damage this would cause, called my friend Patterson to come to meet me too. April didn't know him at the time; oddly, a decade and a half later, they were in the same birthing class in Los Angeles.[61] When he heard her name called, it resounded loudly, since he had heard it in so many stories. He was almost as uncomfortable as I would have been.

As far as I was concerned, this breakup, combined with my not being at college and having everyone abandon me again—at least that's how it felt—took me to the brink of despair. I was inconsolable. I would spend the next few weeks asking to meet up with April, and I would inevitably lose my composure and cry and beg to get back together again. I think I went more than a month without a girlfriend, thinking she would surely want to get back together, after all.

I was . . . I was . . . I realized I was nothing. As mercurial as my rise in popularity my junior year had been, it had crashed even harder during what should have been my freshman year in college. We had already bought tickets to see Sarah McLachlan at the Universal Amphitheatre. We went and it was really awkward. I can remember 99 percent of the opening bands of everyone I have ever seen play live, and I have no idea who opened for her. I swore to hate Sarah McLachlan's music because of April. But I'll be damned if *Fumbling towards Ecstasy* and *Surfacing* aren't really good efforts at blending the Lilith Fair–style, gender-conscious lyrics of Melissa Etheridge and the Indigo Girls with the better pop sensibilities of early Lisa Loeb and Natalie Imbruglia (this is a high compliment, trust me).

I went back to the junior college and started caring a little bit about collecting units. I joined the improv team and made a few friends. I took an intro to speech class and made clever speeches that seemed sincere to the professor but were, in fact, mocking the assignment for those who could read the ironic subtext. One

---

[61] AA: I am so curious about who Patterson is . . .

of the girls that got the jokes started talking to me. She liked good music and smoking weed. She had a close guy friend who was impressed that I knew the name of the drummer of Built to Spill, so I had his blessing. It was back on. I was over April, and onto the next girlfriend. Her name—I swear on my life—was May.

Postscript about April

A note about my relationship with April: we had a "song." Unfortunately, this was common with many of my girlfriends, and they were usually songs I'd let them choose, or I would choose them because I knew they loved them. There was very little sacrifice on my part in any of these relationships. But they got the songs. April and I had "Crash into Me" by the Dave Matthews Band. I fucking *hate* the Dave Matthews Band. My friends couldn't know that was our song. My friends couldn't know that she bought me the album that the song was on, and it was in my glove compartment. A few years later, when Kyle and I were living in LA we had a "bonfire" . . . in a wok on the patio. We burnt the Dave Matthews Band CD and the letter in which she quoted *Pete's Dragon* and dumped me. I'd really like at least one of those two items back.[62]

1. Maya Kim

She was Mangan's sister.[63] We never dated, but she is number one on the list, with a bullet.[64] My wife has, of course, changed my life and is not even in the same category as any girl on this list.[65] But Maya possibly could have changed me, or so I thought. But the relationship almost crushed me. I'll avoid talking about cliché things like "the friend zone." Maya and I were friends. She was smart and cool in a way that made her able to hang out in the back parking lot, without being *too* fond of it. She was cool enough to be coveted by the cool crowd but well-adjusted enough to know that parking lot

---

[62] AA: Thank GOD for the bonfire!

[63] MK: I had to reread *Araby*, by the way, to decide whether this was a good thing or bad.

[64] MK: Really?!

[65] MK: Good job, kinda critical to make this point.

politics and drama are sophomoric.[66] She would hang out with me (you guessed it, at the damn frozen yogurt place, since everything happened around the frozen yogurt place). She laughed at my jokes, told me to work harder at school, and was not all that impressed by my MTV gig. She thought I was a good guy but needed to grow up. Dating her would have probably taken some sacrifice and change on my part, if she would have been dumb enough to date me in the first place. So I liked the *idea* of dating her. In retrospect, she was probably the kind of girl that would have been a good girlfriend for me in my twenties. And I thought she almost was.[67]

She went to a college nearly two thousand miles away. She had a new group of friends and seemed generally happy. But like all kids away at college for the first time, she probably got a little homesick and annoyed with certain things. She would get on AOL chat with me at least once a week, and she would tell me about her friends and roommates and ask about life back home.[68] She would give me the same kind of advice she did in high school. She asked how I was planning to move forward and if I was trying anything to repair old relationships. She was interested in the fact that I had been baptized and was trying to reorder the way I looked at the world.[69] Also, she was single.

Maya came home for spring break during her freshman year, and I asked her if she wanted to hang out. For some reason it only worked out that we could hang out on a day that I had already planned to go to Disneyland with some mutual friends that went to school in Los Angeles. My friends all had annual passes, so it was a normal thing for us to hang out at the theme park for a day. Maya did not have a pass and was not going to throw down a bunch of money for a few hours of churros, waiting in long lines, kiddie rides, and a light parade finale. I told her I had a free ticket that I had been holding on to. After telling her this lie, I drove to the park and bought

---

[66] MK: (Interesting . . . looking back, I think it was actually *acting* as if I didn't care about being "cool," when like most of us, I probably did care.)

[67] MK: You do realize that not even once did I pick up on this or the possibility of it. We were in different "leagues," I thought—not better or worse, and not in a mismatched "1–10" kind of way. More parallel, I guess?

[68] MK: AOL Chat! Whoa . . . that dates us.

[69] MK: I don't remember giving all this "advice" . . . sounds pretty condescending!

one.[70] So we hung out at Disneyland that day. Kyle knew the general contours of my plan, so he arranged to get lost with our other friends from time to time. That way, Maya and I could talk about college, life, and faith. It was a good day. I was charming and self-confident. I figured she probably knew that I knew that she had been signaling something bigger by communicating via AOL chat. When we carpooled back to our cars, where we all initially met, I offered to drive her home. She agreed. Obviously, things were working according to plan.

The drive down to her parents' new place in south Orange County seemed to take forever (it was probably fifteen minutes). My heartbeat was accelerating as we sped along, and I started to feel the lump in my throat. How do I do this? Stay cool? Confirm what I know we both knew?[71] Try the head tilt and lean in? I parked. She got her stuff, and stepped out of the car.

Damn. Okay.

She's outside the car. Think. Do I get out?

I leaned over toward her open door and nervously stopped her with a question.[72]

"So are we . . . like, dating or . . . ?"[73]

She began to laugh, the laugh I used to think was cute and nerdy at the same time.[74] But now this laugh became a wicked cackle.[75] She kept laughing. Sometimes, this plays back in my mind in slow motion. She said something inaudible, covered her mouth in embarrassment, and closed the car door.[76]

---

[70] MK: OK. Stop. I cannot believe you did this! Now I owe you $80 or whatever it cost back then.

[71] MK: Back up. This was not something *I* knew.

[72] MK: This, I remember. Though I was still sitting in the car—or maybe I got out then came back in when you started talking—because I distinctly remember staring at the glove compartment during this horribly awkward scene because there was nowhere else to look!

[73] MK: You led with something about having to jump in a cold pool with two feet . . .

[74] MK: Who is this girl?! So wrong and inappropriate!

[75] MK: Ha!

[76] MK: OK. This I remember too—I said something along the lines of, "A year ago, I would've said yes." Truth. But let's be real, it would've run its course in a few months, maybe? Except you've apparently included this little anecdote in your *Araby* lectures, and now, this.

I sat stunned as I watched her walk past a few cars up to some steps. I was nauseous and embarrassed and wanted to disappear.

As I began to drive away, I lit a cigarette, turned up whatever melancholic music I had in the CD player, and began to cry.[77]

Gazing up into the darkness I saw myself as a creature driven and derided by vanity; and my eyes burned with anguish and anger.[78]

---

[77] MK: Seriously?

[78] *Notes on Dan:*

Do I apologize? Say "You're welcome"? I'm oddly touched that I make "the list," but it's also a little bit disconcerting.

My image of you in high school kind of morphed over time. In the beginning, you were the new guy—a funny guy who was definitely a "drama kid," but for whatever reason, you were able to cross over. And somehow, being that guy made it OK for you to call me "sloppy crack whore," which later became "SCW" when some lady complained about how inappropriate that language was. In retrospect, as I'm typing this, I'm wondering how was this ok?!

It took me a good year or so to realize that you were the guy that always needed to be "on"—I think that to people who knew you (well, to the extent that you let us in), it was obvious that there was a lot of junk underneath that funny guy persona. But I just didn't go there. I remember comments here and there about your parents, a few painful conversations, and from my spoiled Asian kid perspective, I was a little bit impressed and a little bit sympathetic to the fact that you were financially independent(?) . . . and therefore ate Del Taco French fries and BOGO frozen yogurt for lunch.

So . . . I feel like a pretty crappy friend for not seeing beyond that, not knowing about your demons (can I call them that?) and how oppressive they became. Funny, really, that I ended up a psych social worker/therapist, huh?

All this said, I am so proud (since I've apparently always been patronizing and condescending, I can say this, right?) of the person you've become, now that we're on the other side. But way beyond that, I am totally struck by what grace, healing, and redemption look like in "real life"—and Beth Anne's critical role in all of that. So thanks for giving me that, and for the permission to be a part of the journey.

CHAPTER 9

99 Problems

Or, The Chapter about My Wife That Had to Be Rewritten, Deleted, Rewritten, and Quickly Edited before Publication

A Soundtrack for Reading

1. 99 Problems—Jay Z
2. Ugly Love—Eels
3. Blood Stutter—Handsome Ghost
4. Strawberry Swing—Frank Ocean
5. Singing in My Sleep—Semisonic
6. Boys of Summer—Don Henley
7. Making Love Out of Nothing at All—Air Supply
8. The Luckiest—Ben Folds
9. Our Way to Fall—Yo La Tengo
10. Why Should I Care—Diana Krall
11. Pretty Pathetic—Smoking Popes
12. Question—The Old 97's

Note: There's nothing here by Wilco, Pavement, or Belle and Sebastian because I learned after a decade of being married that Beth Anne only pretended to like these bands.

> *It is not a lack of love, but a lack of friendship that makes unhappy marriages.*
>
> —Friedrich Nietzsche

"Shit. I can't finish it. This effing book is going to kill me. The one chapter that might mean more than any of the others is impossible to finish. I am on a fool's errand. This part of my story isn't written; it isn't finished because the relationship isn't over, and it isn't static. Nothing is stopping long enough for me to look at it and write it down. I can't write the chapter about Beth Anne, and it is central to the story and in the very center of the book. I can't even think about other parts because this is the only part I can't put my head around. Fuck."

This is what I told Jeff, in so many words, on the rooftop garden of a hotel in San Diego we were staying at to finish our books.

"What do you want to write?" He asked.

"I have no idea; it is a touchy subject to deal with now. And it is something that I don't really know what to say about that is both true and helpful. Right now, I think I'm going to have to be a fraud or rethink the whole thing."

"Just figure out what you want. And ask her what she wants. And then you can start to develop who you are with what you want."

"I'm on a fucking deadline, Jeff."

"Then write that. Tell the reader you're on a deadline and this story is impossible to tell without Beth Anne, but your story with her isn't over yet. And don't cuss so much in the book."

"I'm fucked."

And then, on Christmas week 2016 (yes, months after the manuscript was due), the tension was resolved, at least for the time being. The point of the chapter was not that Beth Anne was the "final" girlfriend. My ex-girlfriends represented my search for an intimacy that I could not find growing up. The point of the chapter was that Beth Anne was different because there was a real sacrificial love and intimacy. But I wondered if this was still true. We were going through a rough patch, and I can be fatalistic, but I wondered how long we could last in our current state.

The Christmas miracle of 2016 is that I believe, maybe more than ever, that I love her as much as I could love anything. With her, I have intimacy and companionship and goals, and I still screw it up with my poor use of time, lack of communication, and bad decisions. I love my wife, and I don't know how it works moving forward. I'm still in a ditch of my own making, and I can't make sense of it. I'm waiting to figure out aspects of almost everything in my life. But I love her with a kind of deep and vulnerable love that makes me uncomfortable and might make me self-destructive. The philosopher Ian Curtis suggested that love will tear us apart, but he was bested by Ms. P. Benatar who suggested that it was not as fatalistic, but love is a battlefield. Whatever the situation, I have always found the sage L. Richie to be a font of wisdom, and he reminds us that love will find a way.

This chapter has been difficult because my monsters can't seem to leave me alone. And now I realize that marriage is its own monster. Beth Anne is not the monster; rather, the monster is what it always is: the thing I cannot escape. And this monster has, despite a deep love, affected my marriage. My childhood and teen years and search for identity in girlfriends, popularity, and substances are all part of the same monster. So, in various ways, over a span of fifteen years, my marriage has been something with which I find sorrow, self-destruction, and resentment. This would make for a pretty lousy anniversary card. But I think it's the key to getting this right.

I'm not going to belabor the exact issues that plague our marriage; we all have issues, and it is probably not helpful to air them all in the name of transparency. We might understand the quest for love, and maybe we have come to attain some portion of it, in all its folly and joy and heartache and profound happiness. We also know, if we look hard enough, we can see the imperfections and frustrations that can undo the strongest of bonds. For all the intimacy, there is isolation and a foolish but reasonable hope confounded by an irrational despair. How does love survive the onslaught of these opposing foes? How can love and sorrow intermingle with devotion and self-destruction? It's a cosmic battle. It can lead to madness and despair. But I think this story is about having chosen another way. I have chosen to abandon resentment and despair and self-destruction as the end of the story; it may peek its head up and threaten to destroy what we have, but it will not be on the last page. I can't promise perfection, but I can persevere. My marriage, and the intimacy I have in it, might be all I have separating me from a spiral that could lead to the end of everything. If this sounds overly dramatic, I assure you, this is serious as a heart attack. And if this chapter doesn't give me one, there might be hope.

For now, I'm going to tell the story of my wife, my marriage, and the monsters that have haunted me as we have travelled together through addiction, depression, and despair. And we will continue to do so. Till death do us part.

> *I believe a strong woman may be stronger than a man,*
> *particularly if she happens to have love in her heart. I*
> *guess a loving woman is indestructible.*
>
> —John Steinbeck, *East of Eden*

This was the original epigraph to the chapter. I like it. I like Steinbeck. I think it is a delightful sentiment. I have come to realize, in writing this chapter, that I don't think it is true.

Indestructible? Bullshit. We are all on the way to the grave. The earth is going to burn, and we may remain a footnote in the history of the cosmos. So what are we going to do? We aren't going to just push forward to the next episode and hope it is a better one.

This is the key. This is part of the Christmas miracle of 2016.

Instead of living in fear, we will laugh, both in and at the situation. We laugh in the situation because we are free to, and we laugh at the situation because we know there are much bigger monsters waiting to devour us. We can laugh at the current one because it might be much worse, and this one is therefore relatively harmless. Not that whatever we have cultivated in fifteen years can't be bloodied and bruised. It might come to the brink of destruction and seem hopeless. But this monster, the one threatening this intimacy, is one that we can fight together, even when we are fighting each other. We can be unwilling to succumb to it and to allow it to write the last page. If we recognize that we are all doomed eventually, we can laugh at the folly of all our worry. If we know that we are fellow travelers on the way to the grave, we cannot be beat by the things that kill us, because death is unavoidable. And so we beat on against the waves, Gatsby-style, and with a little love in our heart, we can, for a time, be indestructible.

I am still hesitant to write this chapter in a way that I am not with others. Some monsters have seemed tame and defeated, although I have found this to be more perception and hubris. In the early months of 2016, I may have thought that the specter of a failed marriage was one more defeated monster. And then came an avalanche of issues that buried me in work, Beth Anne with fear, and a relationship that had hit the rocks after a few years of smooth sailing. And so, in the exact year that I am finishing this book, things get hard again. Had I finished this on time, before the trip to China, and before the new job and insomnia and host of personal demons, I may have written about my marriage as a final triumph. But Leonard Cohen reminded us that real love is not a victory march, but sometimes only a cold and lonely affirmation of love. It is a song of praise and thanks, but it can be muted, relegated to the mouthing of words you think you can't believe. I'll leave you to read Jeff Mallinson's *Sexy* to understand the Cohen metaphor and marriage.

But before we can get to the sorrow and joy that has created this chapter and the Christmas miracle of 2016, we should start from the beginning.

I've known Beth Anne since I was about fourteen. She was friends with my sister and several people for whom I had little affinity; this is not a slight on my sister, but at fourteen, I wasn't a big fan of most of my family. Beth Anne seemed about as interesting as anything my sister was into, from dated '80s pop in the age of Nirvana to bad coming-of-age movies (*Reality Bites, Singles*) that tried to supplant the teen movie genre perfected by John Hughes. Also, Beth Anne would have known nothing about this. I don't think she was allowed to watch movies and I am certain she didn't own *Nevermind*.[1]

Beth Anne was different in that she came from a stable home and had a deep piety inherited from her grandparents and parents. She

---

[1] BAvV: I could watch movies (PG-13 was the limit), and I certainly didn't own *Nevermind*.

seemed to not care if she didn't go to the dance or the football game. On Saturday nights, she was absent. (She was at church for her dad's contemporary church service.) She wasn't unwelcome; she just didn't make herself known. She was not a nerd or outcast; she just found herself among them most of the time. She seemed both introverted and also expressive. She was as personable as she was guarded. I didn't dig the paradoxes. You've already read what kind of shallow asshole I could be in these years. She was too deep for me.[2]

We didn't hit it off; we didn't even try to, as we kept to our own circles. I remember hearing stories about her piety or her strict parents. I was in the middle of my string of girlfriends and thought that a church youth group would be a good place to find girls. In my town, so many teens went to youth group, it seemed like another opportunity for singles to hang out and flirt. I was having my first brush with faux-celebrity status with some acting gigs and on the radio show I cohosted. I came to this church group on Wednesday night for a number of reasons, but largely because the youth pastor, Tom, listened to me on the radio and mentioned to everyone how the kid in the back corner was actually really funny. I also went because it was a good way to get out of the house. Beth Anne, however, went to youth group because she actually believed in what I thought of as the sky wizard who granted wishes, and so she could sing sappy acoustic songs. I didn't like this place, but any place was better than home. If Tom would mention my comedic and outgoing personality while I remained quiet and brooding, this might lead to some girl liking me. I had my eyes on a few. Beth Anne was certainly not one of them.

Over the next two years, she would see me ascend the heights of meaningless popularity and the melancholy that came when these social statuses were attained and brought little fulfillment. Meanwhile, she continued to pine for the straight-jawed fellow who could play contemporary Christian songs that called for four fret chords (!) that we hacks couldn't play. I could play "Nothing Else Masters" by Metallica and most of Weezer's *Blue Album*, or at least the power chords. I couldn't play the damn Jars of Clay songs or their secular and equally terribly named counterparts, Toad the Wet

---

[2] BAvV: This is an interesting take on me. I don't think it was that complicated. I was just kind of a nerd.

Sprocket. But, despite the stereotypes we had made each other out to be, she wasn't a paragon of virtue, and I wasn't as hopeless as I thought. And we started to hang out once I realized she didn't think my smoking was a damnable offense, and sometimes she smoked cloves. I suppose she was all right.

And then we got married.

It wasn't that fast, and it's a complicated story that involves my general decline in social capital and popular status and her growing into someone who was still in town after our friends moved to college, and someone who wouldn't take my shit.[3] I stuck around town and dated girls from local coffee shops and a few from my old high school. She was ascending in popularity as she lost the perm and jean shorts and started to hang out with us. Instead of being a buzz-kill, she started to earn her reputation as a stable and noncloyingly evangelical who was a genuinely nice person.

One night when Kyle was in town from UCLA we were at a gas station when the following conversation took place:

Person A: You know who is becoming strangely attractive?

Person B: [someone not named Beth Anne]

Person A: No. Beth Anne. Haven't you seen how she's kind of cool now and has a kind of new vibe with her dyed hair and laidback personality?

Person B: Sure. Yeah, I suppose.

To this day, neither Kyle nor I can remember which of us was person A or person B. Kyle has bequeathed me the title of person A, which I believe contributes to my suspicion that he was person A. Why else would he feel the authority to bequeath me the position of person A? Nevertheless, whoever it was, he was right. Beth Anne was like the girl in the teen movie that underwent the transition from nerd to hot girl by essentially just taking off her glasses, redoing her hair, and putting on moderately cool clothes. And she went to college near LA but had to live at home. So she would come to the coffee shop I was

---

[3] BAvV: Actually, this is the beginning of the recurring problem with us. I did take his shit.

working at and give large tips and hang out. I didn't get the sign that this was an early affection for me (although Kyle worked with me in the summer, so it may have been for him . . . that dude is ruining all my romantic stories).

In my lack of collecting college units (I attended a few colleges but could never make it through a class), I began to plot out the next phase of my life. I had come to join the church by now and decided to go to Japan to work with a church and a school. It was going to be me, Kyle, and our friend Kerry. But we needed one more person. Beth Anne's sister, Mindy, who had lived in Japan, was helping me put the trip together and suggested that Beth Anne be the fourth. She had made big strides, and Kyle and I had thought she was cool and becoming attractive, but we wouldn't want to spend that much time with a still somewhat unknown commodity. Mindy probably thought of Kyle as the eligible boyfriend. Mindy and I got along, but Beth Anne had just come off a small list of less than desirable guys. Kyle was stable. Kyle had a good relationship with his family and went to college. Maybe Mindy thought that I was still a bit of a loose cannon, my influence on Kyle and Kerry could lead to trouble, and Beth Anne would keep us on the straight and narrow. Or maybe Mindy just thought her sister would enjoy the trip to Japan. The last is the most likely answer, but I am supposing the first and second were factors somewhere.

I know I have already established that Beth Anne was cool. But not spend-a-month-or-so-in-close-quarters cool. She would proba-bly try to do the stuff we were supposed to do and not use the trip as subterfuge to hang out in Japan and look for CDs that we couldn't get in America.[4] I didn't dislike the idea of Beth Anne coming; I just thought we could get someone who would be less responsible. But in working with her sister, I knew that it was probably inevitable. And I didn't completely hate the idea.

She ended up coming with us. I'll chalk it up to my weakness and fear of confrontation, other girls being unable to come, and providence.

The Japanese family that took us in had an endless supply of melon. I hate melon, and the smell, and the sound of people eating it,

---

[4] BAvV: You were broke so I bought you the Japanese version of Radiohead's *The Bends*.

and I had to put up with it every day, multiple times a day. I shudder just remembering it. I fucking hated melon. Beth Anne loved it. They also ate fish and rice for breakfast. That is brilliant. Beth Anne has never complained more about anything than the smell of fish in the morning. In fifteen years of marriage, I have learned to tolerate and eventually love the melon that Beth Anne loves. She has not learned to love my favorite dish of grilled fish and rice for breakfast. She did however register as Democrat when I did, so she's not completely unwilling to change with me.[5]

We stayed in a small village during a particularly harsh heat-wave. We slept on the floor and sweated through our clothes and taught English and played American music. The Japanese wanted Elvis and the Backstreet Boys, and we were happy to oblige. The trip was somewhat of a blur. I was somewhere in the midst, or near the end, of my most recent drinking binge and love of hoovering up whatever drugs were on the table. This forced bit of sobriety was probably good for me, but I remember the headaches and constant dry mouth. To combat this, I would walk to the end of the road at least a half a dozen times a day to buy mysterious Japanese sodas. Soon, Beth Anne started to join me on these ritual walks to the soda machine. By the end of the trip, we would wait for each other before going to the soda machine. I began to think that I probably wanted to date her. But at that point, the story would have resembled the story with past girlfriends: she likes me, I like being liked, and I have a person that is guaranteed to hang out and listen to me talk. I didn't think of it that way at that point. I could probably rewrite this from hindsight and claim that it was love at first sight or some such romantic bullshit. I hadn't had a girlfriend for a while and thought it was probably time to either start seeing a psychiatrist or have a girlfriend. I did both.

I may have still had cool sideburns and brooded when I smoked, but the suave guy who thought he could snap his fingers and have a girl like Beth Anne come running was gone. Well, you've read the book thus far, so you probably know he never existed. And there was something about Beth Anne that was both attractive and mature. I

---

[5] BAvV: I actually just tolerate melon, nobody likes the smell of fish in the morning, and I am a Democrat. (Sorry Mom and Dad!)

couldn't shake it as we began to pack up to leave for home. We sat in different sections on the plane, and I spent a good deal of the trip writing a sappy letter to her. If e-mails and texts were prominent, then we could probably track these things down. But this note is lost to the ravages of time.[6]

Whatever the letter said, it worked. We went on a date to a place called the Triangle Square (because here in southern California, irony and a false sense of being clever even pervades what we name our shopping centers). We kissed in the parking structure in a borrowed car. The tension was too thick for me to attempt the head tilt and slight lean that beckons the woman to make the next move. I darted my head across the center console like a snake attacking its prey. I'm glad we didn't end up with bloody noses.

Within two years, we were married. The long road to engagement and marriage included but is not limited to the following things:

1. Sitting on a curb during New Year's on the infamous Y2K (nothing happened!) and one of us mumbling something. The other thought they heard "I love you" and responded "I love you too." The one mumbling did not, in fact, say this. The other was embarrassed.[7]
2. I would serenade the other with depressing love songs by Willie Nelson and Chris Isaak. She gave me a Christina Aguilera cassette single (it was for the very underrated "Come on Over") as a birthday present. I made her two mix CDs. One was for late nights and filled with maudlin,

---

[6] DvV: Historians, take note, this was a letter that is crucial to understanding me at the time, and it is lost in fifteen years. Don't think you can write an entire dissertation on someone by collecting a handful of their letters and suppose that is who they are. Also, kids take note, when you write your premature memoirs, you will likely have access to all of the stupid shit you wrote. Be careful, and delete your cookies and cache. And use pseudonyms and Kik.

[7] BAvV: You can just write that I was the person who said "I love you," but I actually whispered "I love you too" because I thought I heard you say it and I didn't want to leave you hanging.

DvV: I couldn't remember who it was, but I'm glad you remember it as a pity "I love you." I'll make this a footnote.

sad, sad, sappy songs, and the one for the morning was filled with catchy hooks and big choruses. I listened to music and thought everyone should, like you take amphetamines and benzos. Your playlists bring you up or down depending on your state. Inside each of the CD's, I quoted Nick Hornby's *High Fidelity*: "Did I listen to pop music because I was miserable? Or was I miserable because I listened to pop music?" The music made me miserable because it jolted me down from any high (to which it had likely elevated me) or spiraling lower than the floor I was then lying on. I still use music like this. This book is made up like a mix tape (apologies to Rob Sheffield). I don't think I could discern enough about anyone to marry them or, hell, drive across the state with them if I hadn't seen a playlist they made or had listened to on repeat. Beth Anne's genius in the Christina Aguilera single is that it is exactly what you would open with for an upbeat mix. Yeah, its cliché and trendy bubble-gum pop. It's also catchy as fuck, with a solid opening call to come on over, to raise our hands in the air, to walk on sunshine, and to get it on.

3. Nevertheless, I stopped talking to her in an attempt to hasten a break up. She called me out on it and dumped me before I could save face by suggesting a mutual break up.

4. I was dumped and deserved it. I was lamely "cheating" on her with a very strong willed Calvinist from the northern part of the state (hereafter: the VSWCFNPS).

Beth Anne and I had been dating for something like nine months, just shy of a record for me sticking around. But I was getting restless at a new college and decided that moving fields was easier than tilling the land. I had an emotional connection with the VSWCFNPS, as well as an immature understanding of my own intellect and the illusion of a rigid orthodoxy. As I began to think about a relationship with the VSWCFNPS, I played the same game that I always played to get out of a relationship: I stopped calling Beth Anne and didn't show up at the coffee shop where we regularly met. When Beth Anne called, I didn't answer the phone. I hid

and hoped she would go away. This would leave me and my conscience free to go after the VSWCFNPS. Japan had been nice, and
that spring had its highlights. But it was time to move on. This was
how the script went.

I drove home one night, late from studying somewhere other
than where Beth Anne and I usually met, and I saw her car parked
outside of my apartment. I luckily saw the car and quickly turned
away and hid at the all-night donut shop down the road. I eventually sneaked home when she got tired of waiting. She called the next
morning, and I was coaxed to the phone and heard from her that I
would be meeting her at the coffee shop in an hour. No excuses. No
running. Shit.

It was a relatively quick meeting; she broke up with me, and
while later accounts had it mutual, or with me making the first
move to dissolve the relationship, I concede the fact that she, in fact,
dumped me. She cut the ties. And I was free. Too free, and this led
to anxiety and dread. I would learn this habit of freedom, anxiety,
and dread as it replayed through my life. This time, I spent the days
and subsequent days lying on a couch in my office with the lights off
listening to R.E.M. and a compilation CD I made called "Sad Songs
for Late Nights."

But now I would move on; incapable of being alone, I asked the
VSWCFNPS out, and she told me that she would go out with me but
that I needed to fly to Sacramento to meet her family. I scraped the
money together for a flight and cheap hotel next to the airport. *This
was the right thing to do*, I thought to myself. She was new and shared
my current orthodoxy and love of the Sacramento-based band Cake.
Bingo. I'm sure this is the foundation of many relationships.

The story about the VSWCFNPS should be recounted as it happened so it can be laid to rest in perpetuity.

I spent the weekend drunk in a crappy hotel near the Sacramento
airport trying to figure out a way to get back together with Beth
Anne. That part of the story is true; I have played with some of the
facts when recounting the story of my epiphany to others. I figured
a little poetic license wouldn't hurt anybody. And then I realized I
needed to write it down and figured poetic license is different from
lying. And everyone involved would read this. So here is how it actually was instead of how I like to tell it.

I walked onto the plane with my CD Discman and headphones. (I've just deleted a section about two pages long on how much I hated the CD Discman. Even the idea that it replaced "walk" with "disc"—it was a CD Walkman, but Sony made sure we didn't call it that.) As I walked down the aisle, the Clint Eastwood–penned "Why Should I Care," sung in a sultry torch-singer style by Diana Krall, started playing. I swear on Saint George and all the Holy Saints that I decided, while walking, and during the first verses of that song, that I was making a terrible mistake and needed to track down Beth Anne and get back together. This all happened.

Now, the story could go: I run off the plane to find her at the airport hoping to catch me. We each get some romantic props in this version—me for leaving the plane, her for coming to the airport. I think I'd like it if she wasn't there. But I tracked her down. It doesn't matter because none of this happened. And I don't ever tell the story that way. We weren't Brandon and Kelly or Tom Hanks and Meg Ryan.

I did fly to Sacramento and found my way, already drunk by midday, to my cheap hotel. Now the story goes in one of the following directions:

A. I call the VSWCFNPS and tell her I missed my flight and spend the long weekend drinking and pining after Beth Anne.
B. I call the VSWCFNPS and ask her to pick me up, but I have resolved to not going out with her but getting Beth Anne back. I spend the long weekend drinking but meeting her family and making out with her in the back of an old Buick.

I like the former story and have told it dozens of times. The latter is the truth.[8] But my decision to try to get back together with Beth Anne was the beginning of a new phase of relationships for me. For the first time ever, I tried to reconcile my stupidity and confess my love and try to grow the fuck up for a girl I cared about. It would

---

[8] BAvV: Holy shit! You've lied to me all these years? I'm not even mad; I'm surprised and a little impressed. Well done, Daniel.

be humbling and scary and way less fun than finding someone new to flirt with, but this was a new day. Sort of.

When I got back home, I spent the early part of that semester avoiding the VSWCFNPS. I tried the breaking up by avoidance method. She came to my apartment, almost daily, and I hid in my bedroom while my roommates covered for me.

The VSWCFNPS eventually found me, and we walked around the apartment complex. I have no idea what we talked about, but I think there was closure. Although I'm sure we kissed back at her doorstep. And then I hid until graduation.

I met Beth Anne at our old coffee shop and asked her to get back together with me. She told me no.[9] This was Maya Kim after Disneyland and April's letter all over again. But she, ever one for telling it straight, told me what an idiot I was.[10]

I, uncharacteristically, kept chasing her. She made good on her word to give me a second chance if I talked with her brother-in-law and parents before she told them that we were going out again. Other things happened. I have been asked not to tell these stories. I will oblige.

Within two years, we were married and moved to Scotland so I could attempt a graduate degree in a field that I hadn't studied as an undergraduate. While we lived there, I would ramp up to what would become a severe drinking problem.

This was the end of phase one. When we moved back to LA, and my addiction took me to the brink, and we scraped by—that was our second phase. I thought that we were possibly wrapping up the third phase now that I am trying to write this. But I was told by Beth Anne that this is now the fourth phase. The third ended with the torrid summer and fall of 2016. The fourth, which I did not yet know existed, lasted until the late winter of 2016. The fifth began with the finishing of this book. I was writing this during the third and fourth phase of our marriage. The book helped usher in the fourth, and the fifth couldn't commence until I finished this. Please do not underestimate what this fucking book has done to me. Keep reading, writing this almost cost me my marriage.

---

[9] BAvV: I didn't say no. I said yes.

[10] BAvV: I never told you that you were an idiot.

The first and second phase cover the period in Scotland through the birth of my son when I was thirty. These were eight years of denial, codependency, and fighting over everything but my drinking. We knew that this was the problem, but neither wanted to face the fact that they were, or was married to, an alcoholic. We left St. Andrews with a medical leave on account of my erratic behavior and our lack of money.[11]

We eventually moved back to LA and lived with friends and in a shit apartment. While we slept one night, the apartment was robbed. Suckers, nothing to find here! However, our only item of worth, my laptop with writing that had not been backed up, was taken. This would put me back even further. I didn't back anything up because we didn't have the Internet in our place and I didn't have the CDs that were supposed to be used for saving important documents. Once again, Sony, F you. Those CDs were crap. Even if I did back up my dissertation, it would have been rendered useless if the CD was not handled like a piece of plutonium. Please extend me a second for my second Sony related note. Have we sufficiently established how bad CDs sucked? Unless you had a high quality sound system, the quality was marginally better than cassettes, and they were initially marketed as indestructible with commercials that demonstrated this by pouring coffee on the top of the CD—did they not think we would find out that a scratch the size of a finger nail scrap would render your fifteen-dollar purchase useless?

Our good friends and my adopted parents would move us back down to Orange County while Beth Anne would work and I would kind of work, and occasionally, work on my dissertation. We eventually moved to an apartment complex in the next town over, where I would eventually hit the point that you read about in the beginning of the book. My addiction had me so wrapped up that I was incapable of working a full week without taking leave. How I never was fired was incredible. It got bad. The story of my life as a drunken professor is in another part of this book. But one particular story is illustrative of our relationship, my drinking, and the nature of our shared memory of this time.

---

[11] BAvV: You never told me you got medical leave.
    DvV: I didn't. And I did it twice.

I had blacked out and vomited whatever I had eaten with bile and blood profusely all over the apartment. When I was shaken awake by her, it looked like a scene out of a horror movie. The memory of it still rattles me. She put me to bed and cleaned up my drunken, grotesque mess. We have never spoken of it since. She had the quiet strength to keep it inside and let me figure out what I was doing on my own. She might consider it enabling, but had she confronted me with some kind of intervention, I may have never gotten sober on my own accord and stayed that way.

What the hell? That is not a story a gentleman would like to tell. But I think it says a lot about Beth Anne. Except she swears that this is, or at least was, a blatant lie and inversion of what actually happened. Beth Anne admits that this occurred but claims that I came to myself and told her to go back into the bedroom while I cleaned the mess. Why do we both have completely different versions of the story? And why are we certain that the other cleaned up the mess and spared the other the embarrassment of the situation? I have no idea; I cannot be the hero of the story. And she claims that she has never brought this up because of my insistence that I take care of it all and she not deal with it. I think maybe each of us sees the cleaning up of this embarrassing mess as the sacrificial act of taking care of a problem we both had.

The third phase was soon to commence. We soon had our first son, and within nine months, I was sober. I was in love with our little boy, and the fear of holding him while drunk and dropping him plagued me as was the fear of developing too close a relationship with him, knowing that my fate was probably an ill-timed accident and death. As he began to move about, he did so with either a menacing look or his arms above his head. This would eventually earn him the now ironic nickname of "monster." Once I started writing this book, that nickname was put to rest. In fact, the reason I don't call him monster is largely because he has helped me fight a very real monster. This began the third and, I thought, the current phase. My sobriety was the conversion of several factors including a late-night talk show host, my favorite podcast, the slow death of a family member due to addiction, and a rash decision to quit drinking and stick with it. My two earlier rash decisions were to get married and to go to graduate school. I must stop thinking things through. My brain has shit for brains. I need to stop listening to it so much. As I became sober, it became clear to me that I was not going to stay sober by white-knuckling my way through the night and events with alcohol being served.

Beth Anne and I began this third phase of our marriage, which could be the first intimate and mature stage of our relationship. We spoke openly about our situation with our son and soon to be second son, and we didn't talk much about my sobriety. We began to learn that we had to trust each other to make it. She had to trust that I wasn't going to revert to the boozehound I had been. (I didn't have a desire to, in all honesty, after a while, but I still had a recklessness that has served to awaken my monsters up to the present day.) I began to realize that Beth Anne was both strong and foolish. But not invincible and not a fool. She would quietly bear some misdeeds of mine and with deliberate intentions allow me to find my own way, sometimes to the detriment of the family. I became sober because I had chosen to and was not cajoled or convinced by her. And so subsequent changes would also have to made by me. I'm still waiting for some of them to abate.

But lest I make this a story about one sinner and one saint, I came to trust her as well. I began to talk about how I felt and thought and my fears of our boys turning into the worst imitations of myself. I had to trust that she cared for me. I had to trust that I had not fucked things up so bad as to lose all credibility with her and others, and ability to take care of my own business and care for the family as a husband and father. We spent six years in this strange new state of foolish, but necessary, trust. It was foolish in that no one should trust another to this extent. It is foolish because the other cannot be completely trustworthy, but you put your faith in them because love believes all things. It is foolish and illusory, and it is necessary. It is the foundation of the fourth phase.

The third phase, the smooth sailing, ended when somewhere along the line, trust begun to break down. The intimacy that marked our relationship and served as the opposition to my addiction began to wean. A particularly brutal summer, which was initially supposed to consist of decompression and rest, became a blur of life changes that had us barely able to stand up straight and deal with the mundane, let alone career and life-altering. This was the fall of my eleventh year as a professor and now assistant dean; it was supposed to be a sabbatical. I had not let up at my job since I started. (Even as a drunk, I had to keep long hours—then to get by and now to keep up with a pile of new responsibilities.) The spring was tough, and the summer ended up a catastrophic disaster with an ill-timed trip to China. Instead of a sabbatical, I left the one job I thought I was made for and took a new job working for a small nonprofit organization as a scholar-in-residence and director of curriculum. This change afforded me a freedom I had never experienced before and, with that freedom, a crippling fear and dread. The fall and early winter were plagued by medication changes, book deadlines, and realities of growing children and navigating our relationship with each other alongside our relationship with our children. While Beth Anne is often the well of hope, she had begun to fall into her old patterns of muddling through, head down, and pressing forward to the next act. I had begun to despair of a happy ending to my own book as the addiction fought to supplant the intimacy that was breaking down as I spent my hours working and a resentment built within both of us. Winter came, and while there were the occasional flashes of our harder times, the end of the year was coming with ominous signs (at least for me). And then the Christmas miracle of 2016.

"I can't write this fucking thing because I don't know where it's going," I complained to Jeff as we looked out over San Diego from the rooftop patio of our hotel.

"What does she want? And who do you want to be?" He was vexing me with the same relationship questions I had thrown at him before. He was being an asshole.

"You can't worry about anything until you decide these questions, and then you can write the chapter," he said coolly as an incarnation of both the Dude from *The Big Lebowski* and a desert shaman, forcing me to realize that my monsters were not killed off in the book but still waiting at the door, desiring to devour me.

"I have no clue, I can't write the end of a story that isn't over, this is a fool's errand," I rebuked him.

"You won't know where the story is going until you know what you want, and she knows what she wants." A few hours after this conversation, I spent hours on the phone with Beth Anne and thus came the Christmas miracle of 2016.

The Christmas miracle of 2016 is in the little details of our conversations and our spoken and tacit agreement that muddling through was not enough. It was an acknowledgment that we had lost an intimacy, and we, despite my maintained sobriety, were thrown back to old patterns of mistrust and distancing ourselves from one another lest everything blow up in our faces. I am not going to make any predictions about how long this phase will last. I'm just going to flow. I'll ride the wave and surf the Tao.

In the meantime, I will accept that the monsters I can't shake might be real and worse than I imagine. I will, with Beth Anne, stomp on the monsters with merriment and refuse to allow them to catch us and hold us captive for the next demon to exploit. We will enjoy life and each other and our boys. We are going to do the things we must, but also the things we love. And we aren't going to bum people the fuck out complaining about the shit that everyone goes through. It might be hard sometimes, but it's also going to be fun. We will metaphorically, and literally, have sex and watch *Star Wars*. We will laugh at the monsters not because we are making light of them but rather because we know there are much worse monsters to come. We will be crushed again, and it could be worse—much worse. But we will not muddle or push through the time of reckoning with our monsters. We will give whatever trouble comes the middle finger by laughing at it too. We do not fear that which can kill the body, destroy our relationship, or all earthly goods. Shit has gone down, and will continue to, but as long as this remains open to revision and refuses to give up hope in the ultimate, we can continue to be baffled, and though beaten, we will remain unbowed. In sickness and health. I hope. And actually hope. It's all we have.

I wrote that last sentence and figured that the chapter was done; I had figured out my marriage and was well on my way to meeting my new deadline. I like the end of that chapter. The telephone call, the resolution, the hope, it all was true and simple. Everything was coming up roses.

Yet I struggled through the next months of a sinus infection, insomnia, a change in medications, and an uncharacteristically cold and wet season. The "Christmas miracle" was a chimera. I had a lot of time to think and answer the question I had asked Beth Anne: "What do you want?" Beth Anne and I fought, but more and more, we kept our distance from each other. On the rooftop call in San Diego, Beth Anne asked me directly, "Do you even like me?" and I took too long a pause. A rot had begun to infect our hearts, and by late January, we were so exasperated with each other that we became roommates passing in the night. A week later, after a series of fuck-ups on my part and what she admits were particularly exasperated and controlling methods to "fix me" again, we had decided that we had had enough. We yelled at each other on the phone and met up for a dinner with some friends. As we left to go to our separate cars, we had another heated conversation. I told her I was leaving and wouldn't be coming back. She didn't fight it. She was numb to everything and hardly cried.[12] I acted like a douchebag and thought, *Finally, freedom. Damn, she was cramping my style and running my life. No thanks, Mom.*

I lived at Jeff's house, and she stayed with the boys at our house. I would come and spend a few days with the boys as she went to hotels or friends' places to stay. I was a wreck with my sinuses and insomnia. Plus, I had resolved myself to the fact that a divorce was inevitable. Every time I spent a few days with the boys, I could only look around the house with a deeply depressed sense of melancholy and dread. I knew either I would have to give her the house or we would sell it and split the money. I didn't want to be a cliché but I subtly, or not too subtly, tried to get a head start on the part of the divorce when the kids decide who they wanted to be with. All I wanted was a 50/50 split and an agreement that didn't sap my already meager bank account.

When we passed off the kids, we only said hello. All texts were short and to the point. I was preparing myself emotionally and mentally for the divorce. She didn't want to divorce, at least then. I was thrown right back into the old habits I had with high school girlfriends. I would have to make sure there was somewhere to land once this was over, and I had to make sure she thought she was dumping me. I couldn't ignore her completely because of the boys. But I could hopefully do something to make her call the whole thing off. We were officially separated and knew it was the right thing. Beth Anne

---

[12] BAvV: In those first few days, I thought if we were going to get divorced, it would be because Dan was an asshole.

knew it was the right thing. It was tragic, but it would have been even more tragic if we stayed together in the state we were in and let that affect the boys.

I had just finished the chapter that stopped after the nice little section on hope and the Christmas miracle. I couldn't have a fuck-up on my record for people to criticize just as I was publicizing the book. I had to admit that the monsters I am still trying to beat are those of my own making, again. I had sedated myself for so long against the reality of marriage and a family with substances and self-isolation. This tour might be less the victorious march around my defeated monsters as much as a new wound, ripped open for me to bleed out on stages across America. But knowing I was getting divorced was a relief. So much damage and so much history of a codependent relationship had sapped both of us. It would be hard telling people and navigating certain things, but what's right is right. Consequences be damned.

And then I got on a plane from Dallas back home. As I sat and listened to music, I started getting contemplative. Would this be a replay of the story about flying to Sacramento almost twenty years earlier? Nope.

I didn't listen to Diana Krall, and as much as I would have loved to start pounding the free drinks in my upgraded seat, I figured that would be even worse for the book. I watched *Blue Valentine* with Ryan Gosling and Michelle Williams. Fuck. You shouldn't watch that movie. Ever. It is to difficult marriages what *Requiem for a Dream* is to heroin and what *28 Days Later* is to zombies. A bad marriage and heroine and zombies are a terrible combination. Luckily, I only had the devastatingly difficult marriage. But as I watched *Blue Valentine*, I realized that maybe, just maybe, I should keep myself open to the possibility of reconciliation. I didn't want to. And I realized it would never happen.

Two days later, I came to get my son for football practice, and as I walked in the sliding glass door, I decided that I wanted Beth Anne back. I didn't want, primarily, my marriage back, or my boys back, or our reputations, or sticking with some of the easier consequences we dealt with already. Beth Anne told her parents, who were remarkably chill about it all. We had travel plans, and the people that arranged it told me not to worry.

But I'm not one for measured and patient actions. I asked her to come in to the back of the house with me. I told her I loved her and that we needed to be back together. It wasn't just a romantic flourish. It wasn't doing anything but possibly opening myself up to more heartache. But three days earlier in Dallas, I was looking for spots to hang myself. Things sucked. And not just because they were inconvenient or I thought about what it would do to my boys. The simple answer to so many of my problems was possibly hiding in plain sight. And when I saw her helping my son get his cleats on for football, wearing a floral print blouse, and with her hair done perfectly in a "doesn't look perfect" kind of way, I may have been a goner. And then I saw her smile at Coert and I became jealous that I would never receive that kind of attention and affection. From her. I could probably find affection, or at least sex, somewhere. If I wanted to, I could try to remarry and have new kids to augment the times I wasn't with my other kids. But I wanted her. I wanted her more than I wanted a good family environment for the boys. I wanted her more than I was afraid of getting tattoo removal done for her name on my upper shoulder. And so I told her. She was hesitant, although she saw this as a happy thing.[13] As of a few days after I turn this into my publisher,

---

[13] BAvV: Now, as we are able to acknowledge what we have done to each other, we face the somewhat daunting task of change. It seems scary. And yet, we pray for peace and the ability to see what needs to be done. Peace. Peace. It was my mantra in the last month, especially as I recognized my need to control. Breathe. Peace. Even in the darkest days, when I didn't know how this story would end, I decided to get my very first tattoo. A dove to represent my prayer for peace.

I hoped we wouldn't get a divorce and thought maybe we would reconcile when Dan called me the day I was going to tell my family that we were separated. We talked about a bunch of things. But one of the things he said to me was that he was thinking he didn't want to live without me.

The day after Dan came home from Dallas to get Coert for football practice, we had another fight. I was trying to control how we would get back together. Same old shit. But he called me on it. Something he rarely does, which was part of the problem. And I saw it. And then he got all romantic on me. He told me I could hurt him again and again and he will never leave me. He's with me to the end. So now I rest, knowing we are in this together, to the end.

We got back together because hope won. We must hope that, in Christ, we can change. But it is more than that. We've talked a lot about the death of our old marriage and the rebirth of something new. Something beautiful. We can listen to music and watch TV together. I hope someday to dance to Yo La Tengo.

I will be moving back home and starting counseling and all the other stuff you're supposed to. I'm not scared. And I don't think she is terribly scared.

"Shit," I thought out loud.

"What?" Jeff asked.

"What do I do about that chapter with Beth Anne now?"

I had taken this whole chapter out and written a weak apology for why I didn't write about her in the book.

"Put it back in with an additional section on what has gone down," he responded.

"I'm on a fucking deadline, Jeff," I responded, curtly.

"When did a deadline ever stop you from doing something in the past?"

Touché.

And thus the chapter went from a slightly manufactured paean to Beth Anne, to the new version with the hastily named "Christmas miracle," to the despairing version that was all of two pages explaining why marriage is hard and I wasn't going to write about mine, to the recovery of the last version with the most recent developments added.

I'm going to stop here and send it to the editor in the next few hours to make sure nothing else goes down and must be added. I think the drama of the past year has coincided with the writing of this book. Both the events and the process of writing this book have fed each other; next time I'm going to write a cookbook.

DvV: Why didn't we dance to Yo La Tengo at our wedding? That's right, I was hopped up on a handful of pills and washed those down with copious amounts of whiskey. I hope the wedding ceremony went well. Also, there was no dancing at our wedding.

CHAPTER 10

Transatlanticism

Or, Life in Scotland, Madness, and Faking It through Grad School

All these songs are written by Scottish artists. This list has been compiled with the help of the greatest musical mind in Scotland: Mr. Stuart Johnston, a.k.a. Disco Stu. We worked together at the Olde Castle Tavern in St. Andrews. The last six songs are his along with his explanatory footnotes.

A Soundtrack for Reading

1. Expectations—Belle and Sebastian

2. Over and Done With—The Proclaimers

3. Act of the Apostle—Stuart Murdoch from *God Help the Girl—Original Motion Picture Soundtrack*

4. Mad Dog 20/20—Teenage Fanclub

5. Only Happy When It Rains—Garbage

6. Saturday Night—Bay City Rollers

7. Sunshine on Leith—The Proclaimers*

8. The Concept—Teenage Fanclub**

9. Rip It Up—Orange Crush

10. Young at Heart—Bluebells

11. Nothing to Be Done—The Pastels

12. Dry the Rain*** —The Beta Band

Notes on the Soundtrack

* Leith is a famous port in the north of Edinburgh and home to Hibernian FC. Hibs, as they are known, are a kind of Boston Red Sox of Scottish football. Last May, they won the Scottish Cup for the first time since 1902. There was a wonderful story in the papers about an old man named Sam Martinez. He was 106, and the last guy alive to see Hibs win the cup. The club took him along to Hampden to see the final against the Rangers. The Leith side won 2–1 in the last minute of the match, and the papers were full of photos of old Sam and his Hibs scarf. Mr. Martinez died a few month later, a very happy man. Hibs fans have sung this ode to love and one's roots in honor of their team for many years (Charlie and Craig from the Proclaimers are both fans of Hibernian FC) and when it's sung by 20,000 football fans, a capella, every football fan in Scotland wishes it was their team's anthem.

** The most Californian song ever written by a Scottish band. This comes from the album *Bandwagonesque*, still in my top five of all time. Dan knows the significance of this album when paired with *Nevermind* . . . right? Last summer, I went on holiday and decided to buy a band T-shirt to strut about in and look cool(er than usual). I paid £15 for a Teenage Fanclub shirt, and I stand by my choice.

*** Sounds neither Scottish nor pop. But it's both. Never have I heard a song so designed to be listened to on one's own. It is the very definition of a "Desert Island" track.

College was the new high school. Graduating from college, let alone high school, seemed inevitable for a middle-class white kid in suburbia. Everyone graduated from high school, and everyone went to college, right? There were a few examples out of the Matthew McConaughey *Dazed and Confused* mold, but they were the exceptions. Since we didn't have Facebook when we were in college, we assumed that everyone must have graduated because . . . well just because. Because that's what you did. We were all the beautiful people, with the right ideals and brains and drive. We were reminded that we were amazing and special. We believed we were brave and intelligent and capable of anything. So we all finished what we started. We were invincible. And, for those of you older folks decrying the younger generations for feeling entitled, please remember it was your generation that taught us this. And we lapped it up.

I graduated from high school with a little help from a kind counselor who made a few bureaucratic difficulties disappear. I barely made it out of high school.

College? It took me a couple years to get acting out of my brain, but I eventually settled down. I ended up graduating with a BA in theology, but I wasn't intending to go into church work. This was like learning to sew with no intention of making or mending clothes. Or, better yet, it was like spending all the money on the perfect full room set from IKEA, bringing it home in pieces, setting everything up, adjusting the particleboard side table, hanging the lights and sconces, unrolling the futon, and laying it perfectly on the carefully assembled rack, and then . . . deciding to sleep in the car. With such behavior, you may well have learned a thing or two about patience, how to make things using instructions without words, but your prior decision to start on the project in the first place kind of nullifies most of that. Plus, it's IKEA. By the time you are in your early thirties, you will loathe it and wonder who the hell shops there. Until you have a kid and the cycle begins again.

I had a degree that impressed a few dozen people at best. Now if you finished your degree in part to impress people, there's a strong temptation to rack up *more* degrees until you have impressed as many people as possible. So I needed more degrees. I certainly had to get out of theology. A BA in the field almost rendered me unhirable outside of my immediate networks. A masters or PhD in the field would give me the opportunity to have maybe an additional eight jobs in the world. So I decided to change my trajectory toward a subject that I hadn't studied formally since my junior year of high school: history.

Despite quitting GATE, getting kicked out of honors classes in junior high for plagiarism, and all the dropping out, I had at least eked together a few skills. I can read. I have a good memory, and I try to organize things and people and ideas so that I might better understand them. There it is! That's my trick! And when my then professor Jeff Mallinson suggested schools, one of them was St. Andrews, which would allow me to transition from theology to history. After submitting a few writing samples and a little bit of fudging about how well I knew German and Latin, I was in to a master's program.

So we were off. (In case you missed it, I was married in 2001, so Beth Anne was coming along.)

St. Andrews is a sleepy village, located in the East Neuk of Scotland. Think of the Eastern seaboard of Scotland—sharing a latitude with Alaska and across the channel from the Netherlands. It is a town without a railway—too tucked into the coast. It is a town without a McDonalds—too historical and proud for a lit-up yellow *M* on its cityscape.

The three roads and a majority of relatively newer buildings were made with the stones from the Cathedral when it was first destroyed by lightning and then by religious fervor during the Reformation (making these relatively "new" buildings about four hundred years old).

The entire town, with small outlying housing tracts, is composed of about twelve thousand people. The university made for over half the population. When the students went home for the summer, the place filled up with golfers heading for golf mecca: the Old Course.

My student housing was in the farthest part of the burgh near the collapsed Cathedral and castle. Above the stone archway, the inscription read 1350 AD. There had been a few upgrades, but it was still drafty and felt medieval (albeit with bad orange carpeting). Out the front window, the view was dominated by the cathedral, or what was left of it. The western entrance, where popes and princes, including Robert the Bruce, would enter in pomp, was immediately in front of us. It was half destroyed, recognizable as something that was once impressive—it was the second most travelled to pilgrimage site in Europe—but now was only a hollowed-out remnant. It was held in by a wall that kept tombstones and the remaining half-structures tied into a whole one. You could enter it until sundown. After that, you would get ushered out for your own good. The absolute darkness, the wind and spittle whipping off the North Sea, and the general ghoulishness of sepulchers and tombs created an atmosphere of dread and fear that, with even a modest imagination, would send you scurrying for the respite of a lamppost or well-lit pub.

In 2002, we had just begun a new century and a new war. The Internet was just good enough to be annoyingly slow. We went to things called "Internet cafes" where we would pay by the hour to use crappy Windows 98 machines and dial-up modems and sip lukewarm coffee, while our Prodigy account loaded with electronic mail that might have been the equivalent of sending something off with a pigeon.

All of this is psychically significant, and there was a global and cultural significance to everything. But much of its glory was lost on me because my hapless Anaheim Angels (then owned by Disney and just coming off of the periwinkle blue pinstripes) had won twenty of twenty-one games behind the bats of guys you'd never heard of (like Kennedy, Eckstein, Spiezio, and Wooten) and on the arms of a suddenly unhittable Jarrod Washburn and rejuvenated Aaron Sele. This was the most unexpected thing in my lifetime, next to the Rams winning a Super Bowl, Gretzky coming to LA, and Magic Johnson contracting AIDS.

When I left for Scotland to gather more degrees, the Angels were in the middle of a four-game series with the division-leading Oakland A's. I must have left on a Thursday, because they were playing a day game to open the series. By the time everything else important happened, I was waiting, impatiently behind a guy at an Internet café, only to finally slip into his still-warm seat to light a Lucky Strike and see that Troy Glaus had gone on a tear and the Angels won three of four and were now leading the division.

The next few months were going to be some of the most important in my career, as I had to impress the fellows that had accepted me and convince them that I could hang in the new discipline and read Latin well enough to pass my exams. I was also living in a new country with a new wife and trying to handle an ever more spiraling addiction.

But the Angels made the playoffs.

You have no idea what kind of emotional pretzel my guts were twisted into.

And the Angels beat the Yankees. And Adam Kennedy's three-homerun game nailed the coffin shut on the Minnesota Twins. So we were finally in the World Series, but I was living in a different country and in a different time zone. I would stay up all night, watching the games from my little television while holding an antenna out the window into the swirling North Sea winds in late October. One hand on the antennae and one on a drink.

I will not regale you with all the details of what turned out to be the highest scoring World Series of all time: the furious game-six comeback and the game seven victory at home, in front of a now bursting-at-the seams park. Seriously! We were there two months earlier, and there were maybe six of us taking up the left field stands. Now this!? Never underestimate how quickly Southern California fans can join a bandwagon.

The morning after the win (which came at about 3 a.m. Scottish time), I was ecstatically running around the quiet cobblestone streets of St. Andrews. Drunks don't need an excuse to drink, but this was an important night. If I usually drank for emotional reasons and their short-term benefits as a clinically depressed addict, well tonight I drank for normal reasons, just like normal people do, though maybe like twelve normal people.

A few hours later, I had to make my way still part drunk, part hung-over, to St. John's House—a building that might outdate all others at the university and is rumored to have been a meeting place of the Knights Templar in the eleventh century. The building was all curvy and windy with stairs and brick walls and weird entrances to rooms you wouldn't know would otherwise exist. They had done some updating, probably in the '70s. It was kind of like Hogwarts, if you imagine Hogwarts three generations after Harry Potter left, and the place was updated with cheap carpet and paint.

I walked up one flight of stairs and through one small cramped room of mailboxes pigeon holes, ducked through another entrance, and then walked through a door where the step was about a foot steeper than normal into a dimly lit teaching space, with all exposed bricks and a few small windows. In the middle of the room, there was a large rectangular table. Our instructor stood by a blackboard. He was bald, with pirate's loop earrings, a felt green overcoat over a tartan necktie, matching kilt, and calf-high army boots. He stared forward in disgust. Maybe he wasn't angry; maybe it was his version of what the kids today call a "resting bitch face." He didn't intend to look mean, but he was terrifying. He would begin Latin instruction first thing each morning by having us pull out a text at random and having us translate it, line by line, student by student. He carried a long cane and would smack it on the table when we conjugated a word incorrectly. His Scottish accent may have been one of the few angry Scottish accents I have ever heard. Scots, like the Swedish, always sound happy regardless of the content of their sentences. But this Latin instructor (known for his works detailing late medieval witch manuals) was a mix between Bruce Willis and Emperor Palpatine. In a kilt. With a scowl.

I sat next to another first-year postgraduate. She told me I looked awful. I tried to explain, to an English person, what it meant that the Angels won the World Series. I should have just said, "My local team beat incredible odds to win their first ever championship." But a mix of being overtired, hungover, and terrified led me to a long whispered explanation of the World Series. This woman, about whom I can remember very little, asked me if I should perhaps go home before class started. I reeked of alcohol and could barely keep my head propped up over my incomplete Latin translations.

The class began with the slow and steadied rapping of the stick on the table, and we were off conjugating. I had not done my work and was hoping that I would get an easy sentence to translate. The professor passed over me, or perhaps he stopped with the translations to meander into a lecture on how the English stole the crown during the Glorious Revolution and would forever be loyal to the Stuarts. I think they still hang people for this in Great Britain.

Whether it was a preternatural gift for remembering things (which, I think is the actual skill most academics have) or a drive that let me stay sober enough to study and write before I passed out, I flew through my Latin class as well as my first-year seminars. I routinely felt sick in the morning—a mixture of getting used to keeping

up with the Scots at my local tavern and then drinking in private
once I got home. But that sickness was also related to my deep fear
that I would be discovered as a fraud. No amount of good marks or
"attaboys" could quell the sneaking suspicion that I didn't belong.

It's not that I have low self-esteem—it's just not a category I
understand. I usually suppose that anyone who compliments me is
doing so to curry favor. St. Andrews was a high watermark in what
could have been an ego-inflating exercise in academic adulation.
Except I couldn't take the compliments. And if anyone knew how
little I worked, they would certainly banish me from their august
ranks.[1]

As that first autumn turned into winter, most of the students
left town for holiday and few golfers came to bear the elements. Beth
Anne and I stayed behind in the sleepy town, now virtually coma-
tose, save the wicked wind, biting cold, and regular dusting of snow.

A cold and dark medieval burgh, once the center of Scottish
religious life, now abandoned by even the students and golfers that
make it a destination throughout the year, made for a metaphor not
lost on me. The sun might rise around noon and scatter just across
the horizon before setting around two. Restaurants would close by
seven from lack of patronage. The few souls you crossed paths with
on the street were too busy pulling their hoods over their heads and
scarves around their faces to acknowledge you. I took to walking around
the town with music in my ears and a parka over my head with
only the red-orange glow of a cigarette protruding from my Gore-Tex
hood. I was still making mix CDs with titles like "It's Getting Dark Early"
and "Darkness Falls." A regular evening consisted of me walking around
the town until I decided on a pub, and then I would sit and work on the
crossword puzzle for a few pints and then wrap up and walk to the next
place. It was, perhaps, the most depressing months of pub crawls ever.
I would always end up back at the Castle Tavern, my home away from
home (although, perhaps my flat deserved that title as this pub was
more my real home). I had a regular seat at the bar and would start up

---

[1] BAvV: Dan will not highlight the fact that he was very well-liked by many in town from
the academics to the townspeople in the pubs and coffee shops. He was very good-natured
and able to laugh at himself, which endeared him to many as grad students tended to be a
little less affable. Obviously they didn't know everything going on behind the scenes (and
I only knew some of it), but on the whole, it seemed like most people took to Dan's vibe.

conversations with the local fishmongers, mill workers, and construction men. After a few drinks (or, a few more, being that I had probably had four or five pints by now from previous establishments), I could start to "talk shite" with the locals. I was something like their strange American friend that could remember lyrics to songs and mediate pub arguments about pop culture trivia; I also put a lot of money in the jukebox—I may have the record, and Bonnie Tyler's "Total Eclipse of the Heart" was easily the most played song.

Among my academic friends, I was fearful of being exposed as a fraud. Not academic enough. Not cut out for it all. Among my friends at the pub, the "townies," I was afraid of being found out as some kind of rigid and condescending academic. Perhaps I felt most comfortable around the ruins, where I routinely sat against the walls and listened to music. The voices in my head would begin to accuse me of being a fraud and of not spending time with my work or my wife, whom I had dragged across the world, only to avoid by walking the lonely streets. I needed the music; I needed Will Oldham or Damien Jurado to drown out my own melancholy and allow me to chew on theirs for a while.

This worked for a while, but if I wasn't careful, the darkness would overtake me. I knew about suicides before. I figured I was too busy, or managing to look busy, to let any of those dark thoughts enter my mind. After all, I had about fifteen people who were impressed with what they believed I was doing. They thought I was conquering the academic world and speeding through a rigorous master's and PhD program. But none of them knew what I was actually doing. I was slowly drinking myself into my first alcoholic cycle whereby I had to keep drinking to avoid my hands from shaking and a massive headache.

One of the darkest moments of my life came on one of my late night, drunken walks around town. I walked as far to the east as possible: right up to the rail and cliff that dropped about one hundred feet straight down into the dark, freezing sea. I had been listening to Johnny Cash's *American Recordings* and especially Cash and Bonnie Prince Billy (Will Oldham) singing "I See a Darkness." It is a hauntingly beautiful song when sung by Bonnie Prince Billy, but when an old, half-blind, and dying Cash begins to warble into the microphone, the hairs on the back of my head stand up. I lit a cigarette, started the song, and then began to look out into the pitch-black night, where the black sea and the black sky made no distinction. This was thousands of miles of cold, deadly, deep sea. It is the equivalent of considering space and noticing that something is likely out there, but realizing how insignificant and weak and nothing you are to it. This darkness will swallow you. As Cash and Oldham sang, I started to gasp for air, quietly at first, and then loud enough that I covered my mouth in case anyone was walking near.

I believed I was a fraud to my wife, who I had brought out here with the intent of giving her an adventure and a respectable husband. I was a fraud to the university, since I knew I couldn't give them the effort that they were asking for. I was a fraud to the guys in the pub, pretending to be "one of them" by outdrinking them and not shitting myself.

I spent one night in the back of a pub that I didn't usually frequent and didn't know any of the regulars. I drank and cried behind my open laptop in the back corner of the pub. I was fucking everything up. I don't remember thinking that, or tying any of my problems to my drinking, but I knew something was deeply wrong and that I had to figure something out quickly. I usually figured it was just regular money issues, or maybe my depression and anxiety flaring up in a new situation.

Everything was in ruins.

I was the cathedral, at once a place carefully crafted for pomp and circumstance—more an indicator of something holy than something actually holy in itself. It was a beautiful mess. And, on my more romantic days of looking back at my disease, I like to see myself as a kind romantic and beautiful wreck.

And then we moved back home and up the road to Los Angeles. Any wishful thinking about romance or beauty gave way to the wreckage. And then things started to spiral.

CHAPTER 11
Monsters

Or, The Chapter about Alcoholism and Some Kind of Recovery

A Soundtrack for Reading

1. Monsters—Band of Horses
2. I See a Darkness—Johnny Cash with Bonnie Prince Billy
3. Lived in Bars—Cat Power
4. Heaven Knows I'm Miserable Now—The Smiths
5. Tom Traubert's Blues (Waltzing Matilda)—Tom Waits
6. Country Feedback—R.E.M.
7. Where Is My Mind?—The Pixies
8. Let Down—Radiohead
9. My Curse—The Afghan Whigs
10. Take Pills—Panda Bear
11. What Were the Chances?—Damien Jurado
12. Untitled #1—Sigur Ròs

"That's impossible!"

I have no idea what I thought was impossible, but the next thirty minutes are as vivid as any in my memory.

"That. Is. Impossible."

"Impossible."

"Impossible."

With my fourth repetition of the word, I may have received a look or two from my friends in the high school parking lot.

"Impossible," I whispered.

"Impossible!" I said it louder, trying to stay in the conversation and add levity to the increasingly frightening situation.

"Impossible," I said again in a lowered tone. I was a class clown, and my penchant for certain alternative comedians may have led many of my peers to think that I was attempting some sort of absurdist joke. But when I turned around and covered my mouth, said "impossible" at least twice more in rapid succession, and then walked off quickly to the rest room, I think they knew that something wasn't right. Almost every conversation that has led to footnotes in the text, or friends who were happy to talk about what was the elephant in my room for some time, acknowledged that I was troubled in ways that most kids weren't. You had the "bad kids," who lashed out at authority and the psychologically troubled kids, who, perhaps due to molestation or abuse, lashed out with bizarre sexual activity and were quickly removed. One of my best friends in high school, and a man I am still in contact with now, told me that he thought there was a deep sadness and worry in my eyes. And while no one seemed more comfortable on stage, I was perpetually uncomfortable in my own skin.

There is a scene in *The Aviator* when Howard Hughes, played by Leonardo DiCaprio, begins to repeat words and phrases over and over. He can't stop himself and has to run off covering his mouth. When I first saw those scenes, a strange wave of fear and comfort washed over me. I had to leave the theatre. I bolted for the exit and started breathing loudly. I walked into the bathroom and then right out the exit. I pushed on the door and stepping in and out before the door could swing back. I walked to the end of the theatre's corridor. I was sure this was psychosomatic, but unfortunately, that didn't make my problem less real. I had been doing these things since before I had ever seen anyone else do them. I think, much like the epiphany a decade later that I had a full-blown alcohol problem, I was suddenly aware that I was suffering from something. This was a thing some-one else did! But it meant what I do is a real problem too.

I may have "fixed" certain things since then. At my worst, I will start to stutter and tick and find a place to hide, preferably on the ground, where I can curl into a fetal position and wait for it to stop. I remember starting to feel weird and prone to oversensitivity and noise when I was around five years old. Someone in my family was eating cereal, and I put a hoodie on and covered my ears. I was yelled at for doing this. For years, I couldn't stand the sound of silverware on ceramic, people eat-ing apples, or people's throats when they take a big drink of something.

I've been running a heavy internal monologue with myself for decades. Often I am mouthing words, shouting at myself in my head, or putting my head into a pillow to stop the multiple voices. I'm told this is common enough and that if it isn't affecting my daily life, it should be fine.

I realize I have been doing this since I can remember. I would touch the wall in my room multiple times before being able to leave. I would stand by the dumpsters in junior high while my hands shook. My inner dialogue would become the mouthing of words to the delight of my classmates, and when I would start repeating the actual words out loud, I would excuse myself to go to the bathroom.

Whether it is the addiction or the depression, a crippling single-mindedness mixed with fear, self-isolating, and attempting to medi-cate myself has always been the norm.

In the past few decades, depression has become almost fashion-able. The label "bipolar" is slapped on anyone with a personality that mirrors the sonic that Nirvana borrowed from the Pixies: the loud-quiet-loud phenomena heard in "Smells Like Teen Spirit," and the Pixies' "Debaser" and "Dead." Anyone who has feelings of euphoria and sadness are welcome to self-diagnose as they will. I don't want to be a serotonin hipster and claim that I was doing it before it was fashionable or that I have the real bona fides. The more we allow our-selves to express the full range of human emotion with others, the healthier we will be. Furthermore, I'd rather more people get them-selves checked out than not due to a social stigma.

Many people have written on depression and done a great job describing what it feels like, medication issues, and the collateral damage it does. Kay Redfield Jamison's *An Unquiet Mind* is, in my opinion, the finest of them all. She is a psychologist herself who not only studied and suffered from spells at my alma mater in Scotland but can explain what is happening in an intensely personal and breezily informative manner. Andrew Solomon's *Noonday Demon* is as well-told a story about crippling depression as a journalist as any I have read.

So there you go. You may have already forked out money for this book and don't want to fork out money for another. Sorry. I'll do my best to give you the rundown of my story and the general feel of living in the shit. This might be for the perspective of you who do not have the fear of this black cloud rushing to envelope you. It may be of service to those of you who do suffer from the same malady as me, that you might see we are all in this together. Wherever you are psychologically, I believe we can all benefit by talking about our own experiences and using language to share our experience, hope, and strength with one another.

Addiction

Alcoholism is some kind of disease. You can play fast and loose with definitions if you want. Maybe it's a disease like cancer. Maybe it's a disease like hoarding. Whatever it is, it doesn't affect just one part of your body or life. Everything gets thrown into the tumble cycle with this thing. The problems an addict faces are typically symptomatic of a larger problem.

My alcoholism, and I stress *my* alcoholism, because I can't get into the heads of other alcoholics, was definitely a symptom of other things. I've got a drinking problem. I'm not an active drinker anymore. But many of the problems that got me liver deep into the cheap booze haven't dissipated over the years since I quit. Except pissing myself. That doesn't happen anymore (although, when incontinence comes with old age, it won't be as shocking as it will be a kind of flashback to my twenties). Except, there was one time I was driving past a dodgy place called City of Industry late at night and didn't want to stop. I made it to a decent looking gas station at about 1 a.m. and thought I could use the restroom, so I let down my mental guard. But no one was around to give me the key chained to a hubcap. (Is there a black market for keys to gas station toilets?) Anyways, no one was there, and so I did a little dance to keep it in. An attendant finally told me that it was open, that no key was necessary. By the time I made it in, I was a second too late. I was heading home, and I know that urine is sterile, so I didn't care that much. But I thought you should know that sometimes even sober guys piss on themselves a little.

Firsthand Account inside an Addled Mind

The following is from a Tumblr account that I created to work through my feelings back in 2008. Please note: I was extremely depressed and very drunk when I wrote this. Putting this text, directly from Tumblr, directly into my book might be the worst idea I have had. I could try to rewrite what it was like then, but I must have wanted myself to see this at some point. I have habitually done things about which I felt guilty, not wanted to admit it, and then done something that might uncover me just in case I felt the sudden urge to confess to someone. Here, I have cut and pasted directly from the site.

I'm not sure what I'm doing to myself. I know that this isn't a good thing. I know that if I were to look at all of this from an objective standpoint, I would say that this might be the stupidest thing I do. I can write excuses. I can say that I have this reason and that reason for doing these things that I hate doing. I could blame my parents or circumstances or whatever. But everyone can blame someone. I suppose everyone can thank someone too.

I need to thank Beth Anne. She should go on and live a life free from the guilt that she would probably feel. Maybe not personal guilt, although I'm sure she would think she was to blame a little. But that's not true. This is about me. Not about anything else but one actor willing to do something that is bad. It wastes what little money we have. It jeopardizes my reputation in a way that could be so damaging I would not recover and I could become a cautionary tale.

Remember Dan? Yeah, we all loved that guy. He was smart and funny and empathetic. And then . . . well, the incident. And even though he probably could have stayed around and fixed it.

Although she, and they would stay around until the bandages came off. This is something that is so deeply shameful that I don't think that I could look at myself or others the same. It could be a good story, like "once I did these bad things, and now I don't." But I don't trust myself to not do these bad things. I think I would do them again. On some level. It could get really depressing, like rubbing alcohol or *My Own Private Idaho/The Basketball Diaries* bad. "Down on the Bus Mall" by the Decemberists is a song that haunts me because I can see my life turning out that way.

How many shadows and shells of people do we see. The homeless guy? Was he always dirty and disheveled and despised by the community? He probably was a kid with problems that turned into an adult with problems. I don't think I can say he or she is morally degenerate and that's why they are the way they are. They got caught in some situation they couldn't help themselves from. And it ended there.

Why don't they kill themselves? I would have to think that if things get that bad, I certainly will. Maybe if I have kids that will change everything. Maybe then I'll be living for something. But I wasn't afraid to fly until I got married and realized that I would be leaving someone behind. I don't need to inflict any more pain. But if she sees it coming, or is prepared for it, then maybe she will ease into the idea of me being gone and then she could live a much fuller life with a husband and family that gives her everything she would need.

Maybe this is why some people have kids? Maybe this is why I am afraid to? If I do, then I'm tethered to them, in a good way, but also in a way that can't be broken. I don't know if Freud or whoever is right, but if you don't know your dad you are probably fucked in some serious ways. Maybe it makes them stronger and some kind of advocate when they grow up. Or it eats them and they follow the same pattern as me because I have given them my genes.

But why am I thinking so responsibly wright now? I should be continuing my downward spiral, but I'm not.

This is something. Keep writing. Don't stop.

There are people to love and there is being loved. And you need both. And I think I need both. But if I'm so fucked up, maybe I don't have the capability to love because my stupid decisions keep me from being trusted, or around. And so people will only love me, if they can, from a distance. And of course, who could I love. Puppies? Orphans who don't know any better? If you aren't loved, can you love someone else as they should be loved?

I see where this is headed.

But can anything stop me from doing this?

Who will save me from this body of death?

I've always like purgatory—that's where I should be. I need to purge, be burned, cleaned, made new so that I don't have all this shit and this inability to say no to something. I can't say no on my own. It's like a plate of cookies, or a bag of candy, I'm going to eat every one of them, whatever my good intentions not to are. Even the Mambas with all that packaging. All those little wrappers that make their way into my pockets and the washing machine.

How much can I ask for forgiveness? What is actual changing—metanoia (Greek for changing mind, going out of, changing the nous).

What if I say, forgive me this, but let me not stop that. What if I stop some of the stuff, but not all of it. That's impossible. I think I've given up everything that wasn't booze. And now I'm screwed. I can't give this up, nor do I know if I have to. But I think I should. I know I should.

I know I should. I know I should. I know I should.

End up in some rehab? Dank AA meetings? Having people whisper about what I did? I haven't killed anyone in a car accident yet. I think if I did, I would do something to kill myself on the spot. Cyanide pills in the back of the teeth. I'd probably try . . . I don't even know. I could get out of the car and drink every fluid I could get out of the car—coolant, oil (I'd have to get under the car?) Maybe that's why some dudes need guns around, so that just in case, they get to end it their way. Because of my lack of foresight with important things, if I had an easy way to end it. I bet I would. And maybe at a bad time. Like when I was just depressed or something.

Can you hear me! I'm shouting here! God, put down your gun, I'm already dead. God, put down your hand. I'm not listening. Maybe someone reads this and wonders who wrote it. It's certainly not going to be publishable, but like the website from the kid in school in Tennessee (?) back when he used to post pictures and song lyrics. It really touched me, and he probably has a mortgage and a job in sales now.

I say, and believe, I don't need to "quit." I think there are other ways and means to get a hold of myself. To come to myself. Or some shit like that. Some desperate measure that doesn't call for a completely drastic decision—or at least the kind I'm supposed to make, but might not have to.

Here's the deal though. It feels good. Or at least it kind of feels good. It doesn't feel bad, and sometimes things feel really bad, and so by doing this, I feel less bad. I don't really know of a time when I was a grown-up and didn't drink. I don't think I could ever not drink. I would have to have some kind of medical procedure, or prohibition would come back. Would I drink if it was illegal? Maybe not. I stopped doing illegal drugs years ago. And that was kind of hard. But I don't now because I probably just don't have the right connections and I can't get that shit in the store.

Here's the simple secret of the plot: I like to drink. I like to lose myself. I like to let my guard down, at least with myself (and sometimes others, although that can be dangerous, I might say too much). Drinking is very popular for a reason. Bars will be around a long time after these dumb juice places go out of business because people realize they could just eat a piece of fucking fruit.

Depression

I've been kicked in the groin and punched in the kidneys. I'm doubled over after a knee jerk into my gut knocks the wind out. I stumble and fall. I'm being held down, not only by the weight now sitting on my chest, but my lack of strength and breath and my fatigue from such a beating.

Nevertheless, he tells me, "Let it go; let it roll off your back."

She says, "If you can stand up, exercise usually works for me when I want to feel better."

Another says, "I know it looks like you're hurt, but this is pretty common. If you don't make it a big deal, it won't be."

Most of the time, I'm too beat to try to say anything; I just lay there, exhausted and unable to form sentences.

But then, she reminds me that "by being like this, it will help you appreciate when you're not so beat up."

I might vomit. I might cry. I might try to get up and punch someone. I'll most likely lay here and try to fall asleep. The darkness of depression is difficult to put into words. It is being crushed in a dark room. It is trying to scrape out of that dark room into a world that is damned and looking to fuck with you. Every good thought you have is met by 5 bad ones that end with you killing someone or yourself.

I can feel like this for days on end. I've gone months before, only to distract my brain with substances to make the pain and dark cloud go away. And then, after I've distracted myself for a while, I find that I am deeper into the mire than when I started what I thought would be an antidote.

According to my psychiatrist, I have a major depressive disorder. That sounds bad. That sounds depressing. That sounds like the equivalent of the check engine light on your car going on. You panic, wonder just how bad it is and assume the worst.

This isn't the blues. This isn't being down in the dumps. This is paralyzing. This, which is usually accompanied by relationship problems and other psychiatric disorders, can leave the one suffering alone. When I told my psychiatrist that I had a drinking problem, and revealed the amount of alcohol I was drinking, he seemed unfazed. I was coming out to him as an alcoholic after he had been treating me for a major depressive disorder and severe anxiety disorder. This is kind of like being manic-depressive, but you're less productive than a manic and more freaked out and paranoid and prone to shakes and ticking than the average depressed person. Good times. He mentioned that usually people who have my concoction of disorders are also addicts. Thanks, man. I could have learned that a while back so that I could watch myself and make sure I didn't develop a problem. Of course, I'm being sarcastic. When things suck, drinking is awesome. Come to think of it, drinking is always awesome. Hence my need to abstain, medicate.

I suppose a cursory read of the chapter about my family tree might have something to do with this. It seems this shit is genetic. Or one hell of a coincidence.

Nevertheless, I'm the guy that is beat up, knocked over, and sat on. I have heard all the advice. I've taken handfuls of pills. I quit drinking, and the despair that is created by knowing you can't stop making things even worse has been lifted. I have started taking my psychiatrist's suggestions and prescriptions. It took a long time to get the prescriptions right. I've been on Paxil, which made me feel like someone was inside my brain screaming at me and caused me to scratch myself so rapidly I wore long sleeves to protect me from myself. I had a nice cocktail of Xanax and Wellbutrin, which seemed to work like a charm, until Zoloft was added and the Paxil stopped working, and well . . . you can reread the beginning first chapter to see how that went. I suppose a golfer gets better by taking thousands of swings, and a pianist plays their scales over and over. It's taken more reps than I'd like to get myself to a place where the norm is not a sense of impending doom. But I'd better not tempt fate. I'm not a pessimist; it's just that shit never seems to work out.

Perhaps I can read what I know now about my brain into the past. Some of it has already been told to you. Did my brain psychology play into my love of maudlin eighties ballads? I'll admit that it might be the case for my love of some of them. I'll lay the blame for my love of certain Phil Collins songs on my mental maladies. I'm not ready to ascribe anything else but musical genius to my love of Richard Marx.

The Doctor Is In

His advice was for me to be quiet. And to take a walk. Maybe try yoga.

And to take enough Klonopin, Prozac, Buspirone, and Lamictal to sedate a band of wild horses.

I was strangely excited to go to a psychiatrist. Not bursting at the seams, Christmas-morning-jumping out of bed, Instagramming myself before walking into his office excited, but I was excited to say whatever I needed to say. I had been to a couple of psychiatrists before, all before I moved away to Scotland, and it was a mess because either I was recommended to them by someone (who I was scared would somehow find out what I said) or I went in trying to score some sweet meds: the kind that make the booze all the more effective.

I know that many have a phobia of seeing a "shrink" or counselor. Maybe it's the brutal honesty required or the close examination under which you will be monitored. Maybe it's like a guy getting a pedicure: it's going to be good, but you don't have the nerve to walk in the door and are afraid others are going to see you. Very likely, if you do decide to see a therapist, you will bargain with yourself and determine to only tell the therapist as much as you think he or she should know. This is pretty easy if you start the relationship off as coolly and detached as possible. It's a safety mechanism, and it might help the whole experience.

I was expecting my current doctor to work me like a salesman—I would insist I didn't need this or that, and he would have me walking out the door having signed up for fifteen things I can't afford and probably won't use.

I walked into Dr. Artin's office (sometime in 2006) shaking, sweating, and trying not to repeat words. I figured he would smell the crazy on me, but I wanted to give him the impression that I only needed a tune-up, not an engine rebuild. He invited me to sit. (No couch? I felt ten times better already.) He didn't offer me water or coffee or tea. He didn't ask me how I was or shake my hand with a condescendingly protruding lower lip.

He was acting no different from an optometrist with a patient who was having trouble reading small print.

When I sat down, he pulled up his computer. (What? Wasn't he just supposed to know the answers and medications?) He looked at me with his deep, understanding eyes. (Seriously, I want to rewrite this, but this is exactly what his eyes look like, and I'm not going to use a thesaurus just to impress you.) He had a wry smile and slowly, after about thirty seconds asked:

"How are you?"

"[Silence] . . . Um . . . fine."

"Then I suppose we can say everything is fixed: this is the easiest appointment of the day." His smile remained, and he went to shuffling papers on his desk.

"Well, not fine like good, but in the way you say that because it is polite."

He kept smiling, and his grin was not at all annoying but rather comforting.

"Are you usually so polite?"

"Yes?"

"So," he said, "you do not feel well."

Of course I do not feel well. Shouldn't there be a question mark in there? Don't talk to me like I have some kind of head cold or stomachache.

"I shake a lot, and get afraid easily, and repeat words, and sometimes I can't stop blinking my eyes and . . ."

"OK, you are a nervous young man."

"I think it's more than that. I get really angry and sad and nothing seems to trigger it." (I didn't mention the sad songs that always triggered it.)

He took out his blood pressure monitor and asked to put it around my bicep.

It was official; this guy was the worst psychiatrist ever. He didn't talk enough, and now he was pretending to be a medical doctor. (I didn't know at this point that he has both a medical degree as well as a PhD in clinical psychology.)

"So, what do you want to do about it?" he asked dryly, with his slight accent and a relaxed smile.

"I'm pretty big on letting doctors decide the best way to fix me."

"So you think you are broken?"

"Of course."

Seriously, I was beginning to think Dr. Artin would be another in a line of doctors I visited once and then avoided calls and scheduled appointments like ex-girlfriends.

I think he sensed my frustration, as he shifted the conversation away from me and into a lecture on the nature of what we know about brain chemistry, depression, anxiety, and medications. This! This is what I was paying for. He talked about what we used to think about the brain and what we know, and think we know, today. He described a few medications that he thought might be helpful and wrote me a prescription to take to the pharmacy.

I got the pills. And none of them worked.

I went back the next week and told him that nothing was working. You can imagine his no-nonsense, but slyly grinning, response to my demand for immediate results.

"Would you like to try something else?" he asked.

"No, I should probably give this stuff some time," I replied.

Dr. Artin was, and is, a master of psychological jui jitsu. He wouldn't tell me to calm down, or be patient, or listen more, or be more honest. Instead, he threw the question, or appropriate answer, back on me to answer.

Talk more, goddamn it. Is it better if I cry?

Alcohol as Symptomatic

So the alcohol is a symptom. Of what? An addictive personality? A desire to blunt my nerves and emotions? I can smoke one cigarette a week with no problem. So maybe I don't have an addictive personality. I have also memorized the first draft pick in the NBA for the last thirty-five years and can spend ten minutes making one cup of coffee. And who the hell doesn't have nerves or emotions? What is my alcoholism symptomatic of? Lousy DNA, an inherited gene or predilection, or something more akin to an allergy?

One of the questions I hear most regularly from "normies" (the dreadfully annoying term we use in AA for nonaddicts) is, "How did you get sober?" It makes sense. They seem analogous to "How did you get that job?" and "How did you get your iCal to synch with your phone and laptop?" and "Where did you get that tattoo?" These are innocuous enough questions that might have relatively simple answers that could help the person asking or on behalf of someone.

There are a few answers that I used to give:

"I stopped drinking."
"It was that or kill myself."
"Hypnotism, wizardry, and blood transfusion."

I have other answers—except all true, but maybe hard to explain:

"Love for my family."
"Fear of losing my job."
"God."
"I stopped drinking."

But, to some extent, I think I can pin it to a tweet. Chris Hardwick of *Nerdist* fame (and a number of chat shows about specific television shows) tweeted a link to a clip that he thought was serious and hilarious. Chris is a recovering alcoholic as well, but I didn't put that together at first. The link was to the opening monologue of the Craig Ferguson chat show. Ferguson was the host of the *Late Late Show* on CBS and was brilliant at turning the convention of the chat show on its ear. One night, after a spate of celebrity overdoses and erratic behavior by others in the news, Ferguson came out to do his monologue and started shooting from the hip. He told the audience, in his delightful Scottish brogue, that he had felt off of his game recently in making jokes about poor celebrities that have been caught up in addiction. We laugh at them, he said, but comedy shouldn't be about kicking people when they are down. He started telling a hilarious and deeply personal story about his own battle with addiction and suicide. It is worth finding on YouTube. Toward the end, he got serious and expressed his deepest sympathy for those who "know one, employ one, work for one," and then he added "and oh, especially to those of you married to one." It hit me in the solar plexus. Repeatedly. I watched the clip on my laptop nightly before I blacked out.

Nobody Walks in LA

We moved back to Southern California in April of 2004, since I landed a resident faculty position at a college in Los Angeles (the one where they filmed *Beverly Hills 90210*). I was excited to move back home, at least to get out of what was a spiraling situation in St. Andrews. My hope was that a change of scenery would make me less depressed, less anxious, less prone to meltdowns and benders.

I had, by this time, ballooned up to a little over 250 pounds (gaining almost 100 pounds over six years), and my friends seemed to worry about me, although I was a narcissist with a one track mind. Get booze. Get enough work done to feel somewhat accomplished. We moved in with some friends, but the situation did not work out, partly on account of my lack of working, Beth Anne's trying to find work, and my continual drinking (quietly, at night on their front patio).

In the transition to L.A., I had temporarily changed doctoral supervisors. The hard-nosed (but actually very kind) Andrew Pettegree had wanted to see my progress, and a friend and lecturer at the university managed to get me into my old flat for the last month of its lease. I, of course, had done no work on my dissertation but figured a good month in St. Andrews by myself would give me the time needed to crank it out and get Andrew's approval.

That month was, as you would expect, a complete train wreck. I spent the money I had and overdrafted on booze—I still owe the Bank of Scotland 500 pounds for that overdraft, and I may very well be on a no-flight list out of Edinburgh. I was drinking through-out the day, every day, only managing to set up one meeting with Andrew during the entire month, where he told me that one idea I had was "jolly good" but that it needed work. The "jolly good" from a titan such as himself was reason for a few pints. The "it needed work" part was reason enough for a few more pints. I started trying to find something, anything that I could control. I decided to start eating broccoli.

I had never eaten it and had a gag reflex. So I made multiple microwave packs a day and ate them until I came to love it. Score 1 for Dan. You're on your way, kid!

It was the cheapest thing I could put in my body that wasn't booze. And when I had to "make room" for more drink, the color and smell was both gruesomely vile and wretched coming back out. The thrice daily exercise in it didn't stop me from drinking or eating broccoli.

I slept in the pub that I used to work at more than a few times. Without a cellphone plan to call home, I could arrange to call Beth Anne when I was in not so bad a shape and assure her that things were going better than expected.

I continued my habit of drunk sleepwalking—something that, at home, Beth Anne was always able to curb by waking up and telling me to lie back down, which I strangely would obey in my somnambulant state. But sleeping on my own, I found myself locked out of my flat a few times. I did this by either leaving my keys and wallet at the pub after it closed, or sleepwalking out of my flat and ending up somewhere outside the building. Once I made it in to the pub as one of the guys was closing and slept on the upholstered bench. I didn't see this as a problem, but rather as kismet. After all, I didn't have a drinking problem. Once I made my way to my office in Saint John's house to a side door that could sometimes be jimmied and pushed open. I slept on the floor in my office, although I awoke up terrified and then had to avoid any professors or colleagues on the winding flights of stairs down to the street level. On one of those days that I had to have the locksmith come over to open the door (how the hell did I explain it to him so many times?), I decided that something needed to change. Something had to be done with this reckless behavior.

So I would go out with a key tied on a band around my wrist. It probably made for some witticisms at the pub. I'm sure I wasn't the first to try this, and so others probably thought I had the brilliant idea just like them.

I came back to Los Angeles to find an apartment that Beth Anne and our dear friends helped us to find. We lived on the east side, close to them, but nowhere near the price range of them. We lived in an apartment building, 1920s art-deco style (and probably last fully cleaned then) and filled with others that seemed to be in a sorry state (of course, I am sure they thought of us as the unsavory neighbors with the drunk guy yelling and chain-smoking). We didn't want to admit that it was a shit hole. We showed it off:

> "Look at the new sink!"
> "Oh, yes, we'll redo all the grouting in the tub."
> "We are so close to things."

We did not, however, leave the apartment alone at night. When Beth Anne got a job as a waitress, I would spend days at my friend Kyle or Kaely's place. I would prod them to drink with me like the good old days, but they had their shit together. I started staying in my own apartment, walking to a coffee shop for the Internet (and the pretense that I would work on my dissertation), stopping for more

Natural Light on the way home, and then turning off the crap TV with the rabbit ears and opening my laptop before Beth Anne came home.

"I got a lot finished today, feeling great about submitting."

Bullshit.

One day, at the only coffee place with free Internet, I looked at a site that told you how many registered sex offenders lived in your neighborhood. A red dot close to your address meant one lived nearby. My browser screen looked like it contracted an instant rash of bright-red circles of various sizes. Apparently, a bigger red circle meant more than one living together. My building had the equivalent of a bright-red pimple centered on it.

I also learned that, decades prior, Charles Bukowski lived on the top floor and drank himself to death. A great writer, ruined by drink. We had one thing in common.

In the meantime, Beth Anne landed a really good job back in Irvine. I had also picked up classes as an adjunct at my alma mater in Irvine. And so our nearly six month routine began in which we would wake up at 4:30 (Beth Anne would, at least) and she'd guide me into our car and drive the fifty miles to Irvine while I slept off the whiskey from the night before. I had thought that by changing drinks, I could control myself. After all, you can't drink as much whiskey as you can beer, although I tried.

I didn't have an office, so while Beth Anne worked, I would go to the park near my college (ironically, the park that I got drunk in as a younger man) and sleep in the car. I would pick her up from work at five and she would drive us home through horrific traffic that took as many as three hours to ravage our way through. By that time at night, my brain and nervous system craved one thing, and as we would sit in traffic, we would fight with a ferocity I have never seen in Beth Anne or myself. We discussed divorce, I pounded dents into the ceiling and door of the old Honda Civic, but we never discussed my drinking.

Later that year, I had decided the real problem was not my drinking, but my laptop. So with the little money we had, I bought a new laptop that was more than our rent. Now that I had the right tool, I was destined to finish.

One morning we both woke to a crashing sound. Someone had broken into our apartment while we were asleep. All they took was my new laptop. Being kids from the suburbs, we called the police. This was the equivalent of complaining about loud music in one of Avon Barksdale's high-rises on *The Wire*.

This theft came up in separate conversations with our older and dear friends the Brothwells. Little did we know how pissed they were when we decided to live in that apartment. The time between when he heard about the robbery and the time his rented U-Haul was in Los Angeles packing our stuff to come and live with them was a blur.

The Beginning of the End

We lived with them for a month, and I remember being surly and quiet on account of the difficulty of getting the required amount of booze in my body. When we had friends arrange to fly out from Scotland to visit us, we managed to scrape together enough money to find a slightly less crappy apartment in Tustin. My car was broken into there, but the police this time at least spent some time asking a few questions and writing a few things down in the event that something showed up.

I remember the next few apartments as primarily patios where I could be alone and drink. It was usually under the pretense of reading or working on something. But the nights would end with me, usually, making it to the bed to pass out and Beth Anne getting up in the morning so she could go to work. I started walking around Tustin in an effort to lose some of the weight I was putting on. But the walk would often end at the bar. I would sit and stare at history books as the words blurred, and I drank another schooner of whatever was on tap. Beth Anne and I would actually go there together on some evenings and get to know the bartenders, who were almost all putting themselves through college and took a liking to Beth Anne's questions about their own lives and my reasonably cheery drunken disposition. On nights I went by myself, I would often find myself going out back for a smoke and sitting down and falling asleep. Having the milk crate I was sitting on kicked or a broom handle in my side would usually wake me, and I could run home. Sometimes I would make it out the front door. Sometimes I would make it home. It is here that, while not hitting rock bottom, I would land in the gutter.

Literally, the gutter on First Street in Tustin was particularly wide, and if I needed to take a quick nap or breather, it was better to curl into the gutter than lie on the sidewalk or the local park where the police did late-night sweeps. I remember one night, after meeting a few students at the bar, lying in the gutter and looking up and laughing.

"Oh, if I was a drunk this would make a good story."

I sat up at night on my back patio finishing off my daily ration of booze. This included whatever I drank after I got home from work to "take the edge off," maybe a beer or two or some cocktails before everyone went to bed. I would then transition outside and begin my routine. I would have extra bottles of vodka and cheap red wine in the wheel well in my trunk, wrapped in towels. I would put those back in the cupboard and drink whatever I had been stocking up. This had to be at least twelve beers and either a bottle and a half of wine and a few vodka Diet Cokes. I was obsessed with always having the right amount so that at least I could be drunk enough to pass out, hopefully in bed. Before I was too gone, I would try to arrange the booze left in the house in such a way that it looked like I had some, but not much.

My evening arrangement consisted of reading a few things online, followed by a movie, and then sometimes some writing—completely incoherent—about how I was failing at work and ruining my life and my marriage. Or I might write that I wanted to channel my interests in directions that didn't make me get up in the morning, or have any responsibilities that required me to be sober so much of the day; these were still the early days of drinking when I would wait until darkness fell before I started drinking during working hours.

My ideal job, then, was to either become a member of the lost generation or a professional drunk. I considered both. But writing took too much brainpower, and my drinking got in the way. I was going to learn how to brew my own beer and become a judge. I was at least a semiambitious drunk.

Things soon began to spiral. I went from having some principles about when and what I used to having no principles at all. We (the anonymous group that I am a part of) tend to stay away from morbid stories for the sake of their morbidity. But there were a few things that took place about which I am deeply ashamed but helped me to realize, after the fact, how bad things had become. I blacked out everything but was usually able to pick up the next day and power through. In the last few years of my life as a full-blown addict, I would take the vodka I had stored in my wheel well and transfer it in a travel mug to my office where I could take a few swigs and then cover up a few fingers of vodka in the mug with coffee. I wasn't doing it recreationally; I was having withdrawals every morning and needed vodka to settle my nerves. I didn't want to do this as there were always risks involved with booze because of the smell. My local bar was usually crawling with miscreants around midday (people like professors blowing off class and work to get drunk in the afternoon). These fellows were usually quick to strike up a talk and figure out if you would be a good connection for substances. I never fell back into the drug scene as (1) it cost too much, (2) it could have gotten me fired, and (3) the risk was far too high.

Don't confuse me with a temperance crusader. Or someone who believes certain substances shouldn't be legal. Weed? Cool. Hallucinogens? Depends. Substances that can be used to improve self-reflection and meditation? Of course. As a Rams season-ticket holder in the cheap seats, I rarely see someone and think, "I hope they haven't had a joint, or things could get messy." If anything, I think alcohol consumption is too high in our country. I've done almost every drug, and none of them is as dangerous as the one I could find on the shelf in the grocery store. Alcohol has led to more deaths than car accidents alone, or by accidental home deaths. But I am still opposed to making it illegal. Coke and meth get their own category as drugs that should be illegal, but more important, anyone who decides on that route will become a tragic figure. They are dumb drugs. And the results alone should keep people far from them.

The last two substances I did were coke and meth. How ironic.

Cocaine, if you're curious, is the single best and worst thing on the planet. The ritual of cutting it up, carefully separating lines, and then meticulously rolling a bill and tooting it up your nose is almost like a sacrament. But fifteen minutes later, your high is gone and you need to get more and find a place where you can do it inconspicuously. It gets more and more expensive the more you need to do, and soon you hate the fact you ever started. I've had friends who have done cocaine for years and needed a lot of rehab and see their lives in shambles for decisions that have consequences that never went away. I quit doing cocaine pretty easily. Partly because it got too hard to find and partly because it's more of a lousy drug that is more trouble than it is worth.

My last real drug experience took place with meth. Even the fact that I started, very occasionally, using it, the last time has seared a pathetic picture in my head. I was in a rental car, getting ready to go into school. I never had the right kind of pipe to smoke it with, so I went on the Internet and found ways people had been successful at covertly taking a hit. Someone liked the converting-a-lightbulb-into-a-pipe method. So I tried that. It took me a few broken lightbulbs to get the hang of it, but when you've got it down, you are good to go.

And so, one fine spring afternoon, I found myself crouching in the back seat of my rental car, ducking low to the floor, and taking hits of meth off a modified light bulb.

That was pretty close to rock bottom.

All of this was only for a little while. But the hard part was that I didn't know that. If I had known that it had an end, not only would I probably have started to look forward to it, I might have started to think of ways in which I could stop. When you are in it, you have no idea that not being in it is an option. And so the cycle continues. And while it is dangerous and harmful to your body and socially stigmatized, I found for myself the worst part was the crippling embarrassment that came with it all. I didn't want to talk about it or be identified as an addict. Whether it is one of their own making or not, addicts need to be treated as having the actual medical malady that they do have. Stop kicking us, maybe. Stop shaming us. Remind us that it will be OK and that millions of people quit addictive substances and behaviors.

On my right inner bicep, I have tattooed "If I Am Lost, It's Only for a Little While," which comes from the Band of Horses song "Monsters." So the significance of this chapter title and the title of the book probably make more sense now. If you've found your way to this little corner of the book, let me tell you something: this is the secret to so much of the shit we all deal with. Identify the bad stuff as the monsters they are. Don't doll them up or make excuses for them. And then, once we've identified the monsters, whether we fight them quickly or in a long protracted battle, we can tell ourselves that no matter how difficult it is, and whether we can defeat the monsters at all, the battle only lasts for a little while. We will spend time lost, but in a little while, we will be found. That's the secret to it all.

I wrote an anonymous piece a while back on a website before anyone knew I was in recovery. I wanted to try to answer the question modestly but with real confidence. I'll finish this chapter with that.

Grace and Addiction—Anonymous

I am an alcoholic. And without getting into all the cliché storytelling (which many of us tend to stay away from), I can write that I am not exactly a "garden variety" alcoholic. I am not the alcoholic that people in the local church of "friendly families and uplifting messages" paint as one (you know, James, who once had a few too many Coors and was slurring his words at the end of the night, or Dale, who has a beer or few every night). I am the blackout drunk. I am the drunk who loses his family, ends up in jail and rehab. I am the drunk that drinks the first hour just to quit the shakes and racing heartbeat (and then the next hours drinking until nothing can penetrate the wall of insecurity and doubt until I blackout and start the process the next day). So you get the idea. Not the "oh, poor guy" kind of drunk, but the "holy crap, he's gonna die" kind of drunk.

And while I use the tense "I am a drunk," I am happy to say that I recently took my five year anniversary off the sauce. I don't currently have a drinking problem, but I could certainly get it back fast.

I am a sober drunk today because I found a place where people understood the depth of sin. Where there wasn't a whiff of judgment. No one harassed me into joining a "new members" group. No one spoke about how great life was going to be, but rather, how we live in a constant struggle as simultaneously saint and sinner.

But the theology there kind of sucks. And we meet in a charismatic church. And it's not a church at all. It's Alcoholics Anonymous. And trust me, the church could learn a lot from the way AA has been operating for the three quarters of a century.

I know, we pray a generic prayer to the "god of our understanding." I know, there is no formal absolution. But I'll be damned if they don't get the fallen nature of humanity better than anyone else. And really get it.

I know various Christian "alternatives" to AA exist. Rick Warren and Saddleback Church have Celebrate Recovery. Celebrate? I would have suggested it be called Endure Recovery. But that wouldn't fit in with its American bent on pulling yourself up by your bootstraps and getting better every day. You can admit your drunkenness, but that's always "before." It's much like the "testimonies" you hear at some churches: the worse the better. So long as it is before (and never again), it's OK to share.

Slip up once or twice, and you find yourself in "accountability meetings" and if you can't shape up, you're out.

AA, the generally deistic and theologically barren group of degenerates, gets the depth of sin. And from there, I can hit up church on Sunday for some absolution. In fact, it's really the only part of church I like. I need to hear that "in the stead and by the command" I am forgiven. The shed blood covers me. And that's enough.

I stick through the service (and by all objective standards, it's a good historic Lutheran church that delivers Christ's forgiveness in Word and Sacrament every Sunday). My attention span sucks, though. And a lot of the guys I know are really into theology. And I can't quite get into it all. I dig that they are into it. And I think I get why it's important, I'm just not wired to talk theology all day. I usually hide out after service and get to my car as fast as I can.

I think the doctrine of "simultaneously saint and sinner" is something any alcoholic can dig. Most alcoholics (of the standard AA variety) tend to believe in something. I think the "God of their understanding" might be a really loving and forgiving god. I just think they made him up.

The historic Christian church has the opposite of the "god of my understanding." I don't get that guy at all. I thought he wanted me to join a committee and "get involved." Maybe the "god of my understanding" as transmitted through a bunch of smiling pastors in Hawaiian shirts wanted me to "fellowship" and be "really committed."

It seems the God of the historic Christian church is the opposite of the "god of my understanding." He forgives the alcoholic. He tells me I am forgiven and owe him no "pledge of faith." I don't tithe or join groups. Frankly, on its best day, my church is like an AA meeting, but with absolution.

Maybe the church can learn something from AA. At those meetings, the people are generally happy to just see you show up and sit in the back. They have the same disease I have and are glad to see that there are others (from successful businessmen to homeless men and women on the dole). They get the real problem of our brokenness and know that we only show up because it's a place where we can talk (only if we want) and listen to how others muddle through. (No victorious living here!)

I think the church is for drunks like me. I wish more churches would borrow a trick or two from AA. And maybe with that, more of us (drunks or those addicted to any other shameful or destructive behavior) might darken the door of the church more often.

Chances are, you know an alcoholic (maybe you are married to one, are related, or are friends with one). Skip all the stuff that promises anything more than the righteousness of Christ as your only hope.

I'll remain anonymous for now. I know I'm just as broken as any. And the stigma of a drinking problem might be less than it was years ago. And I'm sure that many of the readers of this would welcome me to any church function at a church that gets that Christ's blood is our only refuge. But as the church is still filled with the "victorious" and "truly sanctified" that would gossip (masking it as Christian "concern"), I'll continue to slip in the back, hear the words "for you," believe them and continue to muddle through with my only hope being a God, not of my understanding, but of the manger and the cross.

CHAPTER 12

Still Fighting It

Or, Lessons Almost Learned and Where to Go from Here

A Soundtrack for Reading

1. Still Fighting It—Ben Folds

2. It's Alright Now—Bombay Bicycle Club

3. That's the Story of My Life—The Velvet Underground

4. Why Don't You Find Out for Yourself—Morrissey

5. Living Life—Eels

6. These Days—Nico

7. The Shape of Things—Melaena Cadiz

8. Here—Pavement

9. Ladies and Gentlemen We Are Floating in Space—Spiritualized

10. Strange—Built to Spill

11. With Arms Outstretched—Rilo Kiley

12. Everything Is Going to Be Alright—The Temptations

*I believe the children are the future, teach them well
and let them lead the way.*

—Whitney Houston

Good morning, sons, hopefully I see you regularly, and you read this
and think, "Damn, Dad, this is all you ever talk about; do I need to
read it too?"

You don't have to read any of this, but I want to wrap this book up
by telling you, the two most important people in my life next to your
mom, what I think I've learned thus far. And I suppose the reader can
peek into this letter and see what I think all of this means. This book
started out as a darkly humorous story about an anonymous alcoholic professor. It then became a little more serious as I realized that
it needed to carry some weight with it, as the lessons I learned about
hope and despair meant something to me. It ceased to be anonymous
when Jeff convinced me to own the story. It could become a little
more revealing as I left Concordia and had fewer restrictions on relatively minor issues, but ones that could cause trouble as a professor
and administrator. And then it became . . .

It ceased to be a book. At least it ceased to be a traditional book
or memoir. So much transpired during the writing of this book.
From my own career trajectory to my ideas about what I needed to
say rather than what I wanted to say. Toward the end of the project,
I was hit by an avalanche of issues that almost crushed me and made
the book impossible to finish. And as a book in the proper sense,
it has been made impossible to finish. So rather, this has become
more of an artifact than a book. It is a piece of work that reflects four
years of my life from 2013 to 2017. Before I get to the lessons I think
I would like you to take with you, let me explain why this is more of
an artifact than a book.

1. I had no idea that in looking at my past I would discover
just how peculiar my childhood was. I've always said that I didn't
have a particularly bad childhood, and that was good, because it was
particularly long. I thought that was a quick way to deflect any conversation about growing up and place the blame on myself for not
growing up quickly enough. In delving into some of my childhood
memories and events, I started to realize, and my editors realized,
that there were some deeply troubling parts of my young life. While

I left most in, there were a few I took out. It turned out to be more painful than I thought it would be. I ended up taking time to reevaluate who I was, how my early years shaped that, and how I might not be defined or shaped by those things.

2. I didn't think I had much of a point, until I first spoke about my life as an addict, and hours before my talk, I decided to frame the talk along the lines of hope vs. despair and peace vs. madness. I had only bits of my book written. When my session began, I read the first part and hadn't really arranged the second part of my reading as if I didn't have a script. I riffed on a few bits I knew were decent but, even now, listening to it makes me cringe. But I received a response that I wasn't expecting. It wasn't just an "attaboy" or "thank for being brave and sharing," it was a room that seemed to catch something of the fire in my belly that made me need to write this. I wrote this for myself, and then for you two, and then I figured some people would read it and have their opinions. That room, with our friends the Mallinsons and Brewers and Winrichs and a host of others from across the country, gave me the kind of encouragement that made finishing this thing possible. It almost wasn't finished. I thought about tossing it about six months before I finished it. I had three decent-sized suicidal moments when I was confident that I couldn't make it through the day. And then, as you know or read, Mom and I got separated. This was on the heels of resigning from my job and starting the job with the podcast and publishers. I had enough problems in the last year of writing this book that I think I could bang out a sequel, *Monsters 2: Bigger Badder and So Incredibly Uncomfortable You Probably Shouldn't Read It.*

This isn't a book about advice or tips or validation if some of the stories happen to resemble you. This book is about hope and peace in the face of madness and despair.

It is the kind of hope that, while dangerous, offers the possibility of a glimpse into the transcendent. It is the kind of hope found in a personal creator God who becomes a baby in the soft green wood of a manger and then a sacrifice for all humans on the dried rotting old wood of a cross. We can get sober without this, and knowing it doesn't make you a superior person. But if there is an actual meaning to everything, we can take comfort in this vale of tears.

I can only remember getting two pieces of advice from my dad, and I think they were really bad. Ask me sometime about them, and

I'll tell them to you privately. You might have noticed I've not written about your grandparents in this book. And you might not know why. The reader might not know either, but I figure that's OK. You can all draw your own conclusions.

So what does this whole book mean? What's the point? It isn't necessarily a tell-all, except maybe me telling you a lot about me. The book is about addiction and ex-girlfriends, in the same way *Charlie's Angels* was a show about law enforcement. This book and Jeff's book, which was released on the same day, are about the same thing. We use the themes of sex and addiction to point ourselves and the readers to a reality that is beyond us.

If you do something really impressive, be proud for a moment and move on. Stop trying to be impressive. If you are, you are. If you try too hard, you're probably only trying to impress yourself, and that is not only impossible; it will kill you. The point about trying to look impressive is that you are probably trying to hold on to something. You are probably trying to find meaning in that one thing. And trust me, it won't work.

There are several ways to try to look impressive. Almost all of them will leave you empty and hurting.

I tried finding hope or happiness as a kid, and it never worked out. That sounds bleak, but it was my roll of the dice. I hope we can give you a home where you don't need to try to impress us and where happiness and hope stomp on the heads of these monsters. Even when things were shitty, we have hopefully kept you calm and not let you be terrified about things you can't control. Learn to hope about things in this penultimate world as well as things in that final world to come.

The second takeaway was to see the danger of despair. It wasn't just giving up on something or deciding it wasn't your thing, but rather it is a kind of giving up on life. It is considering the eyes of the visible world where people crush one another in order to get a step ahead and say, "Oh, well. It doesn't have to be me; I'll try again next time." This infuriates people, because we aren't hardwired to act that way.

The third takeaway is the danger of being taken away by madness. Madness isn't the same as being subsumed by mental illness; rather, it is finding the evil and tragic in this life and letting it write the narrative for you. Madness comes from both a lack of conviction and a realization of what the world is actually like. That is, you know how bad things are, but you are paralyzed in taking a stand against the absurd. Failure to have any courage or convictions will lead you into either a quiet and painful agnosticism or an angry and absolutist worldview that will not allow for any uncertainty or ambiguous propositions.

The answer to this is peace. On my thirty-eighth birthday, you and your mom got me a framed poster that read:

Datta.
Dayadhvam.
Damyata.
Shantih
Shantih
Shantih

This is from the end of T. S. Eliot's *The Waste Land*. This is my favorite poem and one of my favorite pieces of literature. It is chaotic and wild, coming out of the first World War, and with the scattered scenes and pathetic characters, Eliot is playing with the Upanishads and the New Testament. The first three words mean "giving," "compassion," and "control." These are the things that mark the upright person. But the final word, repeated three times, means "peace." Eliot made a reference to Philippians where Paul gives the benediction praying for the "peace that passes all understanding."

The peace that passes all understanding, Shantih, Shalom—all of these are meant to be strong words of comfort. In the midst of a raging storm or amid ominous shaking mountains and unfamiliar refrain, these words of peace reflected a view that everything was safe. Everyone was OK.

Some people chanted shantih or shalom or peace right into the shallow watery graves or until a boulder came speeding down the mountain and crushed them. Even still, they were singing shantih, shalom, peace.

How could they do this? This is where hope and peace are put to the test. Only in the face of absurdity and anxiety and death can we see what our picture of the world looks like. I have never been threatened by a squall or fled rockslides during an earthquake. But I can tell you that with any mention of the word *addiction*, my spine tingles. And while many of the ex-girlfriends I contacted about help with this book were very kind, I still flinch a bit when I hear any of their names mentioned. And so, I have gone into the sea, in the path of boulders, and more important, deep into my own psyche over the past four years.

Tonight, I am sending this book to the publishers. Tonight, I will retire as a memoirist. But if I've opened my chest and invited everyone to come see inside to poke and prod, I think I can also redeem the end by writing something to you both and possibly wrapping this whole project up in a "what did we learn" kind of way.

We can start bullet-point style and move into some bigger points from there.

- Sorry about your grandparents. But you probably wouldn't know what they looked like. The sins of the son should not have the consequences passed down to the grandkids. Then again, I did fine without them (just a little damaged perhaps).
- I don't want to get too dark, but in the three times I've contemplated suicide because no other option seemed viable, I have ultimately not done it because of you two. About a month before I submitted this book, I considered getting in a car and disappearing. But you two made that just a fleeting thought.
- I've told you both that I love you almost every day you have been alive, certainly every day I have seen you. I mean this. Sometimes I wish we could pack you off to a boarding school, and other times I've called a babysitter to watch you and pretended I had plans just to get some space. But this has not diminished my love for you. And my love for your mother is the same. And we have fucked up way worse than you two, but we love by forgiving.
- You can say whatever words you choose. Just be careful of the context. There are no bad letter combinations and

sounds. If you have questions about bad words, please see comedians Louis C. K. and George Carlin.
- Be careful with sex. Read Mr. Jeff's book. Or his forthcoming *Sexy: For Kids!* with illustrations by Jez Tuya.

Now my last point is the secret to the book. It is fair game for everyone. Sorry, kids, you're going to have to share your old man with the forty other people who are reading this book.

Everything sucks, everyone is incompetent, all corporations want to screw you, the church will run you through the ringer almost as bad as the university will, your president doesn't care about you, you can never be popular enough, and there's always someone smarter than you and cooler than you and funnier than you and more attractive than you.

If you are popular, enjoy it. Although, that's hard because you have to maintain whatever it is that got you popular and hope that no one takes shots at you that can expose you as a fraud. But remember, they want to get to where you might be because they don't want to be exposed as frauds.

Put your trust or hope or confidence in anything, and it will eventually crush you.

Please don't think that I don't think you can't trust things. You should. I'm not a conspiracy theorist; I tend to think the government does have the general welfare in mind with many of their laws. If you are popular, enjoy it and see if you might spread the circle out wider to bring more people in. If you are generally incompetent or crap at work or can't make it anywhere on time, remember that most people are, and by changing those things or at least working on them, you can succeed.

In my life, I put all of my self-worth and trust and picture of the world in one basket at a time, only to have it break and for me to end up in the gutter not knowing what was up. It made me angry, and that anger only stalled me from getting on with my life in a new direction or with a different mind-set.

Don't put all your hope and trust in your family. Maybe your parents are awesome. And grandparents and cousins. You're like a regular

Brook Titus living on a compound with four generations of families. But then maybe you want to read chapter 2 again. And please know that I was trying to be as polite and circumspect as possible. I've got some more stories, and they are tragic. Don't make your family an idol. Appreciate it, cherish your loved ones, spend time with them, but realize they are some of the idiots that then go out and make life hell for other people. I'm not assigning blame; I'm just playing the odds.

Don't put all of your hope in popularity and fame. First, who knows you're going to get it? I hadn't made peace with my senior yearbook until my early thirties when I realized that for all the popularity and television gigs and the numerous notes from friends in my yearbook to "not forget me when you're famous" or "see you on the Tonight Show," and so on, and my agent, MTV, comedy and radio gigs meant the world to me, and now they are nothing. Most of the money was either "borrowed" and never returned (it's a fun story) or I blew it on booze and substances and import singles from Japan.

Don't trust religion. I don't mean disbelieve anyone who tries to talk to you about God and cosmos. I don't mean that you shouldn't join any religious affiliated group or join a church. You can get as involved as you want. I think you should get involved. But don't trust the parts of it that seem to only exist to inflate egos, line pockets, and cement hierarchies.

But if you can, find an organization that teaches things that seem backward and astonishingly simple and countercultural and refuses to worship you. These places have existed throughout history. There are two things that have not made it into this book. I almost put them in but didn't. Maybe the next book, *Monsters: For Kids* illustrated by Emily Kimbell, can include them. These two things are very difficult, and only one person knows about them. And he runs a church. And no, he didn't find out and call me in to berate me. I went to him because I knew he was the only person I could tell and not be judged. He's been tasked by his master not to break the bruised reed or put out the flickering wick. He listened and then told me it was OK. It wasn't OK, technically. Those actions and the detestable actions of us all, from the beginning of time couldn't be passed over if we were to have any sense of justice. And so, while we're still far off . . .

Epilogue

Good Friday

It is the spring of 2016, and I am at a park down near the beach. It is seventy degrees and sunny. It is all seemingly incongruent for this day away from the office and rare noon church service. I have the day off, and I am with my wife and two boys, eating lunch at a picnic table and playing. The park is popular, filled with a swarm of children climbing on pristine new playground equipment, manicured grass, and an ocean view. There are what seems to be a group of upper-class, suburban mothers chatting just below the din of their children shouting and laughing.

And then, it starts to happen. Men and women in their twenties to forties start to descend on the open air grass portion of the park. They come in unmarked white vans. As they pile out of the cars, they've got their smokes in one hand and energy drinks or generic coffee cups in the other. This is not a homogenous group, but there are a lot of sweatpants and baseball caps, and a lot of those not-quite-beards that look like week-old five-o'clock shadows. There is also a sense of camaraderie and ebullient weariness. I recognize them immediately. These are my people. These are recovering addicts. This is one of those group home activities that usually take place in the early morning or late afternoon when you have to (or want to) leave the center but don't have any other plans. Usually it involves a lot of sitting in pairs (sponsors or people who came into the program with you); sometimes there is an unfortunate acoustic guitar. But everybody, despite how rough they might look, has the look of someone who knows that somehow they've been given another chance and that maybe things will be better today than they were yesterday.

Near the playground equipment, some of the parents don't notice what's going on or at least politely don't seem like they do. Other parents, quite obviously, round up their children and either have them play closer to their blankets or begin to pack up their belongings.

I am sitting on a bench with a cinematographer's view of everything unfolding. Seeing the kids (including my six- and three-year-old) in the foreground and these somewhat haggard and down-but-not-out addicts in the background show a contrasting picture of present of possibilities and hope but also of the dangers of addiction, dreams deferred and then wasted.

But the addicts in the background—shirtless guys, tattoos of varying aesthetic quality, dyed hair with three inches of dark roots—do not represent the despair in contrast with the "innocence" of the children in the foreground.

The contrast is blurrier than that.

The future of possibilities and crippling disease blend together.

I feel a strange anxiety looking at the small kids with their tanned and well-to-do mothers and nannies.

Maybe these kids will live the lives of privilege they seemed destined to have, with big homes and offices, with big windows and people who bring them coffee. Maybe they will have privately tutored children with perfect, orthodonticized teeth who will inherit both their genes and their portfolios.

But the addicts in the background may be grown-up versions of the "innocent" kids in the foreground. The kids in the foreground might have one story. They might never get (or need) a second chance. This might be a happy accident. Or, maybe they don't die from obvious addictions or a self-inflicted bullet to the head—but they might endure something worse. They might be recognizing the diminishing returns of their daily lives, worshipping their own good looks, wealth, or good fortune. Maybe they have an addiction to holding jealousies, grudges, and secrets. As their stocks and good looks fade, they might die little, daily, painful deaths that are perhaps worse than if they did end up prematurely in the hospital or the morgue.

I'm not suggesting that this is the fate of these children or even most children living in places with parents who take them to manicured parks and allow them the freedom to be children. In fact, it might be less likely.

But those addicts in the background are an embodiment of a hope just as real as the possibilities of the children in the foreground.

Maybe even more so.

Getting it right the first time seems usually an illusion; getting a second (or third, or fourth) chance is rarely illusory. It takes work to get extra chances. It takes hard work through incredibly dark nights and the admitting of embarrassing failures that are almost impossible to bear.

The parallel is, for me, palpable. The children haven't a care in the world. And in a sense, we addicts don't either.

Naïve as it might be for the time being, we all think that everything is going to be OK.

Photo Album

There are very few pictures of me as a kid due to a house fire that destroyed many photos. This is from 1984, when I was five years old. I was practicing a kind of contempt and ironic distance from things long before it was cool.

In high school with Kyle. We graduated in 1997, hence posing here. I am wearing dumb glasses and a cape. Seriously. This is what I did. My insecurities and self-consciousness made me incapable of actually smiling in pictures throughout my adolescence and early years of adulthood.

The black felt prom outfit. Twenty years later, when I was reminiscing with my friend Nicole, who also dressed up in these ridiculous clothes as part of our prom group, she pulled up a photo of herself dressed up in these clothes. Apparently we both think these are important photos to have ready to show when people can't believe how dumb we actually looked.

In Japan in 1999 with Beth Anne and Kyle. Beth Anne and I weren't dating yet but spent most of our time together. Please note how I sat close enough to her to brush shoulders in a lame excuse to brush her shoulder and her leaning into me.

In Los Angeles at my apartment. Notice Beth Anne looking at me with affection. We were not dating at this point, and she would often come to the apartment to hang out, and I would conveniently excuse myself. This is because I was a jerk and an idiot.

Taken in 2012 in our tenth year of marriage. We were pretty happy then, as I had two years of sobriety and we started dealing with our problems.

Beth Anne and the boys. Note Coert's hair, and if you look closely, you might see the drool dripping off Raymond's face.

Me and my boys in 2015.

Me with cohost Jeff Mallinson recording an episode of our podcast, *Virtue in the Wasteland*.

My family in 2013. This was right before the next four years of pain and struggle that writing this book caused.

Made in the USA
San Bernardino, CA
14 July 2017